The Pitfalls of Reform

Its Incompatibility with Actual Improvement

John Tanner

ROWMAN & LITTLEFIELD EDUCATION
A division of
ROWMAN & LITTLEFIELD
Lanham • Boulder • New York • Toronto • Plymouth, UK

KH

Published by Rowman & Littlefield Education
A division of Rowman & Littlefield
4501 Forbes Boulevard, Suite 200, Lanham, Maryland 20706
www.rowman.com

10 Thornbury Road, Plymouth PL6 7PP, United Kingdom

British Library Cataloguing in Publication Information Available

Library of Congress Cataloging-in-Publication Data

Library of Congress Cataloging-in-Publication Data Available
ISBN 978-1-61048-922-5 (cloth : alk. paper) -- ISBN 978-1-61048-923-2 (pbk. : alk. paper) -- ISBN
978-1-61048-924-9 (electronic)

♾ ™ The paper used in this publication meets the minimum requirements of American
National Standard for Information Sciences Permanence of Paper for Printed Library
Materials, ANSI/NISO Z39.48-1992.

Printed in the United States of America

9/8/15

For Madeline and all our kids

Contents

Foreword

Five minutes after first meeting John Tanner some years back, he informed me that his intentions were to change the world. I wholeheartedly endorsed his intention then and even offered to join in his efforts; this thoughtful book is certainly a step in that direction.

Creating a better public education system has become almost a national obsession—and with good reason. Plausible claims can be made that a high-quality public education system is the key driver for our economy, will preserve our democracy through the development of an educated voting public, provides our best hope to realize equity of opportunity and results for all Americans, and enables individuals to realize personal fulfillment.

This obsession has led to significant efforts from the classroom to districts to state education agencies to an increasing role for the federal government. Commitment to improvement remains high.

Unfortunately, and as is discussed by John in this work, research and reasoning lag behind many of the improvement initiatives, operating from personal experience, research drawn from other fields of study—or most troublesome—picking and choosing palatable portions of research while leaving behind politically difficult or economically costly changes that are integral to success. We end up with policies that mandate changes in behavior while assuming that improvement can be achieved by refining our singular efforts—and that the core of the system is correct. In reality, as John points out, the system is organizationally and philosophically flawed, and no amount of improvement in singular areas will change the overall outcomes.

At the core of John's thesis is a basic concern with the notions of accountability sweeping the nation. John comes at this from a highly knowledgeable perspective, having worked his entire career in testing. He knows the field of standardized testing, having been in it. His insights and opinions are highly knowledgeable and respected. He is not an outsider taking angry shots at a troublesome system; he is one of the creators of standardized testing questioning how it is currently being used and for what purposes. As such, his views demand our attention.

Student assessment is not the same as system accountability. Assessing students and gaining an understanding regarding what they know or are able to do is a vital component of accountability, but it is the easiest part of accountability. Once we know where students stand in their learning, the harder part is understanding why we are seeing the results we are seeing. Why is one gender performing better than the other? Why do some of our English-language learners excel when others do not? Answers to these questions enable teachers to change, hone, and refine practice to produce better results. And answers to these questions are not available through standardized testing.

John takes a fundamentally different look at teachers than that seen in most of the current accountability debate. Instead of blaming teachers, John identifies the faults in our system of education that make the job of teaching—and the success we hope for students—almost impossible to realize, going so far as to note that "teachers are actually succeeding at a much greater rate than we have a right to expect given that so much of the system actually runs counter to their success." While the quality of instructional practice can always improve (in the same way that the quality of medical care can improve or the political functioning of Congress can improve), the reasons for the lack of overall success in our educational system are not the fault of individual teachers, but rather the organizational design of the system.

As John logically lays out, we have established an accountability system based on the premise that rising standardized test scores indicates overall system improvement—even as these tests fail to measure the fullness of the learning experience, tend to operate at lower levels of cognitive demand, and were never designed for such actions. Even more problematic, originally designed as a system check—not a check on individual student progress—rising test scores have been assumed to always indicate a higher-quality learning system, when in reality, rising test scores can often indicate more rote memorization and increased strategies to teach to the test.

In many cases, success as measured through rising test scores is actually a false positive of successful changes in practice and better learning for students.

John also digs into the problematic results of the sanctions that are used within accountability systems based solely on test scores. He carefully takes the reader through an explanation of why standardized test scores almost always mirror the demographics of the students taking these test scores—essentially because standardized tests are designed to do so. When schools with high numbers of students living in poverty are shown to be poor performers—as expected by the design of the test—these students are placed into learning environments focused on lower-level skills. Instead of rich and engaged learning, the students who most need our help get less.

Meanwhile, schools with students from higher socioeconomic means demonstrate success—using the same instructional patterns and quality as the previous school—and these students get to experience full, rich, and thoughtful curriculum. This reality, planned by the design of the test, is inherently wrong.

This book is not against assessment or accountability; rather, John takes the time to point out that we need assessment and accountability, but that the way we have designed these systems is inherently flawed. For example, John comments that

> a standardized test instrument—in the hands of a thoughtful researcher—is actually a reasonable tool for helping us understand the degree to which the nature of the disparity changes over time.

> But as an accountability tool a standardized test is astonishingly shortsighted. Remember that a standardized test says nothing about educational quality—by design. It cannot comment upon its cause or any reason for a change.

> It cannot say if a low score is the result of an impoverished school, or what the next step should be if the school wants to experience success. It cannot tell a high-performing school what to do to maintain its standing. If it did comment on educational quality, it would no longer be a fair test because now the scores would say something about a school being "good" or "bad" and any such correlation to such judgments has been carefully and painstakingly removed so that the test can be free of such bias.

> It can show a distribution of students within a domain, and that is it. The reasons for why a school or a student lands at some point in the distribution are completely external to the measure.

This is the core of John's contention: standardized tests are not inherently bad, but the function of using them for accountability purposes creates problems that actually force teachers to operate in ways that run counter to the laudable intention of policymakers who have created our current accountability systems. Ironically, there is little difference in what we all want—better learning for students—but the systemic strategies we have put in place are actually causing achievement gaps to widen and overall learning to decrease.

Ever the educator, John uses the latter parts of this book to talk about solutions. Having thoroughly noted the historical context of our current system of accountability, which in many ways rose from the findings published in *A Nation at Risk*, John has previously led the reader through the flaws of "reform" for a system by only using politically or economically easy solutions. In the final sections of the book, John proposes fundamentally redesigning schools by focusing specifically on the constraints of the system, rather than trying to design around the constraints.

What sounds like an odd strategy becomes clearly intriguing and one filled with possibility as John outlines how such actions enable schools to create learning systems that overcome these constraints. For example, schools of today are largely bound by time. Schools start and end at a set time with a set number of days. Within this framework of constancy, students enter with different levels of proficiency with the expectation that over the same amount of time some students who have previously struggled will learn more and catch up with their peers. As expected, when the amount of time for learning is the same for all students, the actual amount of learning that takes place varies considerably.

Conversely, John's idea is to design the school around time. In this way, time becomes the driver for the school, and as such, it becomes flexible and stops being a constraint. What becomes inflexible—even perhaps a constraint—is the learning proficiency of students. Now instead of ensuring all students are in school for the same amount of time, the system focuses on the levels of proficiency by flexibly bending and moving time toward this end. By focusing on the use of time—rather than assuming it is constant—the time barrier disappears because the school is designed around it and not beholden to it.

Even more interestingly, instead of using a metric looking at the percentage of students who pass a standardized test on a specific day, accountability measures could shift to the percentage of students who demonstrate performance—whenever.

John also offers a series of suggestions for metrics we could use to measure success rather than standardized test scores. For John, a valuable metric is one that not only measures success but also drives actions within an organization. John, who proposes that standardized tests should operate "in the background" and not as a driver for schools, argues that striving for test scores actually decreases behaviors by teachers that can improve learning. Rather, he proposes such metrics as the percentage of students who attend two- or four-year colleges, enroll in the armed services, enroll in industry-certified programs, or are hired for a job.

While one could argue the merits of specific pieces of this example, the intention is to look at the results of students engaging with the public education system and to create a metric where everyone in the system can see a role for their efforts. Unlike test scores where only tested area teachers play a role, everyone, even support staff, can encourage students to engage in these noted outcomes.

The timing of this book is crucial. With the recent publication of the Common Core for English/Language Arts and Mathematics, the Next Generation Science Standards, and the anticipated national assessments that align with these standards, we stand at a new age of standardized testing. Navigating between appropriate and helpful use of these standards and assessments with real learning for students will require us to review and reanalyze our use of the results of these assessments. John's ideas pertaining to this can help us sort through these ideas.

This is a book that offers a new theory regarding educational accountability, and as a theory, these ideas are not the final word on these topics, and John says as much in the process of sharing his ideas. But these ideas provide strong explanations for the current situation we face in education and provide a pathway for potential solutions. It is a book well worth the time spent to read and one that can fundamentally reshape our thinking about how to improve learning for students across the country.

David Ruff
Executive Director, Great Schools Partnership
Portland, Maine
July 2013

Introduction

What if someone in a position of power insists you build a building that is pretty much guaranteed to fall down, threatens you with losing your job if you don't build it, and after it is built and starts to crumble points to you as the source of the failure? And what if they made it all the worse by insisting you do it with tools that aren't even intended for the task?

You'd be frustrated and angry, and rightfully so.

Our current school accountability package in place in our public elementary, middle, and high schools creates just such a building. Policymakers, frustrated with what they saw in education, placed school accountability squarely within the tools of reading and math tests and little else. After all, they reasoned, good schools did well on such tests, and if everyone did well on such tests, why, then, that would mean that all schools would be good.

The simple fact is that such tests are tools that fail to work as designed once you put the burden of accountability on them. Tests meant to operate in the background as a check on a system are now made to operate front and center and are presumed to say something well beyond and in addition to their design.

It is as if policymakers hoped for some magical transmogrification to occur that made test scores mean what they never have just because they declared it so. But they selected the wrong tools for the job, and all the wishing in the world cannot change that fact.

Regardless of the facts, policymakers put in place a system to punish schools that fail to see test scores rise even though the test scores no longer mean what they once did, under the patently false premise that rising test scores (that may no longer mean what they once did) will *always* be evidence of good things happening in schools. Most recently, because those test scores that now don't mean much have failed to rise meteorically, policymakers—

who couldn't possibly be wrong in their reliance on instruments designed for an entirely different, even antithetical, purpose—are now blaming teachers and accusing them of not doing their jobs properly.

How in the world did we get here? And more importantly, what do we do to get to a better place?

■ ■ ■

The chapters that follow will make several points regarding educational accountability in its current form:

1. It is a system that when broken down and explored will be seen to actually work against its goal of educating all students to a very high level.
2. It is a system that creates differentiated expectations for students such that it risks leaving intact the very status quo it purports to want to change.
3. It is a system that risks offering definitions of school and student success that are at odds with each other.
4. It is a system that actually works counter to what those who put it in place intended because they selected the tools that were familiar and convenient, not the ones that were right for the job.

Whether to a parent, a policymaker, an educator, or just a concerned citizen, the consequences of even a single point above being shown to be true are severe. Education represents one of the single largest investments we make as a society, and we make that investment under the explicit agreement that the educational community will prepare the students entrusted to them for the world they are to someday inherit and lead. If we have somehow—whether inadvertently or otherwise—insisted on a definition that runs counter to the goal, we have a right and a need to know.

■ ■ ■

Given the various audiences that may read this, it warrants an aside regarding what we call school reform and the resultant accountability systems that have been placed on our schools. I'll spend a great deal of time explaining both terms more fully in what follows, but an introduction may be useful to audiences not familiar with their actual workings.

School reform is a phrase used regularly by those within the educational community who believe that the educational system needs to be fundamentally changed for the better. Under the auspices of school reform come the three pieces of the reform package: standards for what students should know and be able to do, tests that purport to assess how effectively teachers taught and students learned the assigned material, and an accountability decision that attempts to assign a judgment as to whether or not the teacher, the school, and the broader system were effective at the process of educating each student.

At the heart of the school reform movement is the idea that schools are going to have to be forced to accept a whole host of changes, since schools are themselves at the heart of the educational problems that allowed for as strong a term as *reform* to be the main descriptor regarding the nature of the changes that are to be made. Accountability is the means by which the thumbscrews will be applied so that the goals of school reformers can be realized.

Such strong terms imply that someone has the answers for how to make things better and that they are so confident in those answers that they will force implementation of the system as they designed it and presume that any failure is the result of others.

Supporting the idea of school reform and the resultant accountability package, however, is a flimsy logic that I hope to reveal in the following pages.

Consider just one set of ramifications if the logic is actually flimsy: if a standardized test score—which is the primary indicator in the accountability system—is the means by which quality is judged in a school, that means that a very important assumption is at work: that rising test scores are always an indicator that the school producing them is doing its job.

However, rising test scores can be indicative of either a teach-to-the-test mentality, which damages a student's long-term chances by teaching within the limitations of a standardized test (which is much more limited than most people realize), or a policy of ignoring the test, doing what is right for each student, and teaching well and richly.

The fact is that our present accountability package does not differentiate between the two approaches to teaching. So long as the scores head up (absent outright cheating), the assumption is that the school did right by its students. An accountability system that cannot differentiate between good and bad teaching as a part of the formula is one that should never have been considered in the first place. Under the auspices of "reform," however, it remains a sacrosanct piece of the system.

The three pieces of the reform package are so sacrosanct that no one seems inclined to question their *form* from within the policy community. Our attempts to improve upon the educational standards, to make better tests, and to hold the system accountable all take the position that the design of each part is more than adequate, that all we need in each is some fine tuning, and that having done so the system is primed to produce greatness.

At no point have I seen a meaningful discussion at that level regarding the form our standards take, the assumptions underlying a standardized test, or whether school accountability leads to better choices by teachers. I'll show through the course of this book that in their present state our standards, our assessments, and our accountability systems together promote a system that actually runs counter to the goals they claim to support.

■ ■ ■

Part of the reason it is so difficult to move in a new direction in education— in addition to the sheer size and scope of the challenge—is that the whole enterprise is by any measure riddled with complexity. The systems are complex. The way they interrelate is complex. Kids themselves are incredibly complex. And the entire enterprise has so many moving parts that knowing where to start so that a meaningful change can actually take place can be a mind-numbing exercise in itself.

My goal in writing this book is to unravel some of that complexity in a few key areas such that the underlying nature of these areas is exposed for all to see. Once that nature is understood, it is my hope that *not* changing becomes untenable. At the same time, in opening up some new space in which educational change is seen as necessary, I also want to limit the opportunity for policymakers to continue their shortsighted approaches.

I want to point out that they ought to avoid using tools that they don't understand to police an environment for which they have almost no knowledge. I'm not suggesting that we should just up and do away with the making of educational policy, but rather, that when policy is made it should admit that complex problems require more than just simple solutions.

Regarding the changes that need to be made, though, it is important to realize that it doesn't *all* need to change. Systems theories (and education is indeed a system) are based upon the idea that if you find the right things to change that the rest of the system will fall in line. If it doesn't fall in line, then you didn't pick the right things, or the right forms of those things.

An objective perspective would have to insist that we rethink the parts and pieces that make up the educational package, since they don't seem to have had the desired effect. Yes, scores on the National Assessment of Educational Progress (NAEP) trickled upward over that time, and yes, we finally started paying attention to populations that had historically found themselves to be a marginalized group, but the data on its own doesn't show that something *transformative* has occurred.

At the very least, we should rethink the form of those parts and pieces to see if doing so helps us find what is in the way of achieving the larger goal. But such perspective is hard to find. The actual assumptions being taken at present by those driving the systems of education are that the system is fine, the form of the parts and pieces is right, and the problem is in the implementation. Since the reform movement began, most of the changes have been in the form of tweaks only, meaning that what emerges time and time again is just more of the same in a revised version.

What follows is an exposition on two sets of theories: one that is currently at the heart of educational reform and its accompanying accountability systems, and a different set of theories that I find answer a host of questions that the present working theory cannot. In science, the nature of a theory has little to do with rightness or wrongness: one can never, after all, *prove* a theory. That would require an infinite number of tests to validate every possibility.

Rather, a theory is valid if it explains existing behavior without injecting bias. When a theory does this, it is still only accepted until a better explanation comes along. Even today, there is no single theory that explains the whole of physics. Einstein's theory of relativity explains massive bodies, solar systems, and more, but it fails to explain things on a microscopic scale. Quantum mechanics explains interactions at such a microscopic level that we can never actually see the interactions, but the predictability from quantum mechanics provides the foundation for the entire electronics industry.

Both theories are valid because of their power to explain and predict things, but they are also temporary, in that they possess within them the ability to step aside when other theories that can explain even more can be put forward.

The point is that our educational accountability systems as they presently exist contain a set of theories. That means they hold within them the possibility of being invalid, of not being able to explain much or predict anything. If that is the case, then it is time for a new set of theories that can do what the old ones could not. I offer this book under the auspices of being a theory, but one that does in fact explain far more than those that have been institutionalized in our school accountability systems as they stand.

In the end, this book is all about exposing several fallacies that exist in the theories behind educational reform as well as in the resulting accountability package, but also presenting a new set of theories as well. The fallacies in the present system leave all of us at risk of supporting a system that is designed to fail and assigning the blame for failure to those responsible for implementing it. It would be one thing if we were talking about a business or an industry, but we are not. We are talking about the education of the fifty-five million students that enter our public schools each fall, and that are the future of this nation.

The cost of getting education wrong is sufficiently huge that it warrants a very critical look at what we have done to see if it matches our intent. If it does, then we can all be confident in the path and move forward with a renewed level of commitment to the process. If it does not—and I put it to you that it does not—then a great deal is at stake, and we would be wise to take heed and consider a different direction.

I

Changes to the Educational Improvement Formula

Many aspects of the educational system and the formulas behind it now function within paradigms that have become so ubiquitous as to move beyond question. Rather like the personal computer or the cell phone, we can no longer imagine what it would be like to live in the modern world without them.

Our paradigmatic view of the world has shifted as these technologies have come to take a place in our daily lives, but because the particular shift in paradigms has been so sudden we can still remember a yesteryear and cite specific examples of how the technology has in fact impacted us.

I typed my high school papers on a typewriter, learned to do accounting by hand, and remember when you used to get yelled at by your parents for tying up the only phone line in the house. By the time I finished graduate school I had my own computer, and so did virtually everyone around me. Today, most middle school students have a personal cell phone and a Facebook account.

Most paradigmatic shifts, as Thomas Kuhn reminds us, happen such that we hardly notice the shift until suddenly one day we find ourselves in the midst of a new environment and can hardly remember how we got there or what the former world resembled. It isn't that our memories are suddenly wiped clean or that we are forbidden from ever thinking in the old way again, but rather, that something new has replaced something old and going back is not an option.[1]

The paradigms in which we live and breathe and work are never quiet. They present us with a set of assumptions that for all intents and purposes appear invisible to the naked eye, but it's a bit of a trick. However invisible they may appear, they are still there, humming along in the background, with a sufficient amount of weight and power that they can guide a whole host of human behaviors and thoughts without appearing to lift a finger.

That's the nature of a paradigm: it guides what we do and how we think, often without even being aware of it.

Awareness of the paradigms in which we live is critical if we are to attempt meaningful change. Paradigms contain systems of concepts as well as thoughts that enable a host of activities while also establishing limits that help define the system. When a paradigm shifts from embracing one system of concepts to another, one of the things that changes is that it is no longer necessary to think in yesterday's terms. We can, of course, but yesterday's terms don't mean what they once did and aren't nearly as useful as they once were.

One of the most famous examples of this occurred once Galileo confirmed Copernicus's claims that Earth revolved around the sun. From that moment forward the Ptolemaic and long-held Christian traditions that had things the other way around became impossible to defend. But what was also lost was the centuries-old position of human beings occupying the centermost point in the universe.

Earth and its inhabitants all of a sudden no longer occupied the preeminent position theologians presumed had been established for us, and everyone had to come to grips with the new way of thinking. A step toward a more accurate physical model of the universe was accompanied by a step away from the spiritual understanding of our place within it, and once taken it was simply not possible to go back.

It isn't that we can no longer see or discuss the idea that people once thought that the sun revolved around Earth but that such an idea doesn't mean what it once did.

All paradigmatic shifts are like this. All such shifts move us from one place where thinking is both enabled and limited by the prevailing assumptions for how things are to a new place where different modes of thinking enable and limit different modes of thought. We can always attempt to see old ways of thinking, but we need to recognize that they will mean something different than what they once did, which is why such explorations are always a bit tricky.

Education is in the midst of what we will likely, at some point in the future, view as a set of paradigmatic shifts. We have made the attempt to move away from a system of education that doled out educational success such that it correlated almost perfectly with one's socioeconomic status to one where the goal, at least, is that such things no longer matter.

We have attempted to escape the tests that everyone in my generation and for generations before me took in school and to replace them with something more useful. We have attempted to get control of the content our children learn so that those with the actual responsibility of providing that education choose it and it is no longer controlled by the publishing industry.[2] And we now attempt to impose accountability for success against both the content and the tests onto the educational community with a tenacious ferocity under the assumption that doing so is both necessary and helpful.

I think we owe it to ourselves to submit these ideas to a careful and thoughtful examination to see if the new way of thinking offers an improvement over the old, or if perhaps thinking so is just wishful thinking. I would argue that understanding these shifts at the moment when we are in the midst of them is imperative to see that they truly offer the real and meaningful improvements in our educational system that are the reasons for promoting the change in the first place.

NOTES

1. Thomas S. Kuhn, *The Structure of Scientific Revolutions, Second Edition* (Chicago: University of Chicago Press, 1970), 43–44.

2. In referencing the publishing industry, I don't mean to suggest that they were attempting to monopolize content or make that determination in a manner that was unhelpful to students. Rather, they were in the business of publishing content and had to have some criteria for what to include, and without national consensus documents they were left on their own. Many of them selected content based upon the advice from scholars and researchers, and many good texts were made available as a result. Nevertheless, it was clear that the content was being selected by organizations designed to turn a profit. Moving the selection of content to an environment in which that was no longer to be the case was desirable not just to education as a whole but to many of the publishers as well. They made their money publishing books, and if someone else took care of defining the content, that was one step they no longer had to accomplish on their own dime.

Chapter One

The Educational Formula

The broad formula for educating students at its highest level has changed very little over time, and it is key to understanding the arguments regarding changes in education. It looks something like this:

Expectations for Students

+

Good Teaching

+

Evidence of Success

=

Academically Prepared Students

That formula must, of course, be surrounded by a variety of supports including teachers, communities, and funding, all of which contribute to the process.

The thing that changes over time is how the formula is applied. For example, in the past the full force of the formula applied only to elite groups and ignored certain minority populations altogether, and much of the evaluation process was highly subjective and applied in as many different ways as there are schools. In addition, expectations differed depending on where students lived, as did definitions of academic preparedness.

The history of education can be seen as one that has at different times attempted to work on various parts of the formula. Some efforts go after the expectations component, at times attempting to ensure that high expectations extend to all students and at times attempting to ensure that the expectations are standardized within a system. Evidentiary systems have endured numerous changes, which have included at various times grading systems, standardized tests, or portfolios of student work.

The ideas of what an academically prepared student is have never been stable. Is it a student capable of showing a minimum proficiency in core subjects, or a student fully prepared for work or higher education?

The debates about how education should be carried out will never be completely resolved. The educating of a human being is a seriously complicated thing, and to think that we can exhaust the subject is foolish.

It is imperative for our purpose here to look at the current incantation of the formula. In fact, it is imperative that we consider two incantations of the formula: the one that education reformers believe they are attempting to implement, and the one that is actually being implemented in our schools.

The formula that at present is being attempted is this:

Rich, Common Expectations for Students

+

Great Teaching

+

Success on Assessments That Require Students to Demonstrate Those Expectations

=

Academically Prepared Students

This formula claims that the ongoing standards movement has provided us with the rich expectations. It argues that testing programs now required in every state offer the chance for students to demonstrate those expectations, and that students who do are prepared for the worlds of college and work that lie ahead, which is the current incantation for "academically prepared students."

However, I would argue that the formula being applied is much closer to this:

Content Standards in Reading and Math

+

Teaching Focused on Tested Content

+

Success on Standardized Tests

=

Students That Are Pretty Good at Taking Tests

After all, the formal requirement is for content standards in reading and math, we hold schools and students accountable to standardized test scores in those subjects, and in the end we have an entire generation of students trained on standardized test content and, in a frighteningly large number of schools, not much else. I will make these points in far greater detail in the chapters to come.

For now we need only to point out that most of those at the policy or leadership level working on the educational formula truly believe they are operating within the intended formula. This belief offers an ideal position from which to work. After all, if those responsible for the formula can pretend to have hit on the right formula, then failure is someone else's fault. Failure is not the result of the system, but of those attempting to implement it.

Some parts to the system may certainly need tweaking, so the logic continues (the notion of common standards as opposed to state-by-state standards, which is now a movement that is in full swing, for example), but the issue is with those trying to implement the system, and not with the system itself.

Chapter Two

The Paradigm of School Reform

While the basic educational formula has remained pretty much intact for as long as anyone can remember, the manner in which the various parts and pieces are defined and have been implemented has varied a great deal. The most recent advocates of change have named themselves school reformers, providing a powerful platform from which to drive and promote change. The term *reform* needs to be explored because it serves as the driving force behind many of the changes and yet has enabled a form of change that likely wasn't intended.

The philosopher Richard Rorty put the problem this way: "Interesting philosophy," he says, "is rarely an examination of the pros and cons of a thesis. Usually it is, implicitly or explicitly, a contest between an entrenched vocabulary which has become a nuisance and a half-formed new vocabulary that vaguely promises great things."[1] We need to explore the promise in new terms such as *reform* in order to understand what is in fact being offered in those promises.

Rorty speaks to the difference of working from a position that something is fundamentally broken and in need of repair and a position of being in a state of constant improvement. He suggests a very specific reason as to why the constant improvement position is more appropriate when trying to solve problems: it recognizes at every point along the way that the process is always incomplete and refuses to allow us to ever think we might finally, truly, have the answer.

It is the difference between the idea that a utopian state exists and it is up to us to find it and the idea that sometimes things are so complex that understanding isn't a reasonable goal. In those instances, however, improvement is always possible and always a worthwhile thing to attempt.[2]

5

For educational purposes this is an important distinction. Educating a child is perhaps one of the most complex activities we undertake as human beings, and to think that the solution is ever complete underestimates that complexity.

Working from a position that a thing is always inherently incomplete requires that at various moments in time we must rid ourselves of descriptions or feelings regarding the thing being good or bad so that we can ask, honestly, what can be done to make the thing better. It requires us to admit that while we don't have all the answers, we can offer a compelling reason for the answers we do have. This isn't to be seen as utopian or idealistic, as in practice such distance is pretty much impossible to create, but rather as a principled way to consider change.

When it comes to offering an improvement within such an environment, we don't need to convince anyone that what went before was bad or even in need of improvement, but rather, we can simply make an argument that lays out the merits of the improved state. If the argument can be made such that it compels others to feel similarly, then not making the change becomes irrational and the process required to make the improvement can be undertaken.

Convincing someone that something is broken and now demands an entirely new line of attack requires a very different approach, generally requiring damning evidence and a set of arguments as to why it is unfixable. To convince someone that something is broken, therefore, requires that you have some vision for what things should ultimately look like, and that you cannot see a path of constant improvement within the present system that can get us to that point.

The challenge in declaring a thing broken is twofold: to convince an audience that the thing is beyond repair, and, that a solution exists much closer to an identified ideal state. In education it is perfectly understandable to think that some sort of ideal state exists: a point at which all students can and will achieve at very high levels regardless of socioeconomic backgrounds, race, gender, and other factors. In fact, given that we entrust our children's future to education, it would be illogical and unwise (though it is the truth) for the system of education to say, "Thanks for your child, we don't have all the answers, but we'll do the best we can."

Thus, when education is seen to not have all the answers it is deemed a logical thing to declare the system broken because it cannot guarantee in any state to meet its promise to all children as of some date certain.

It should not come as a surprise, then, that when it comes to improving our schools, a decision was made some years back to work from the position that schools were broken and in need of repair, and thus in their current state they were beyond the ability to improve on their own.

Consider the opening to the 1983 report *A Nation at Risk* that effectively launched the paradigm of education in which we still operate today:

All, regardless of race or class or economic status, are entitled to a fair chance and to the tools for developing their individual powers of mind and spirit to the utmost. This promise means that all children by virtue of their own efforts, competently guided, can hope to attain the mature and informed judgement [*sic*] needed to secure gainful employment, and to manage their own lives, thereby serving not only their own interests but also the progress of society itself.[3]

However idealistic such a statement may be, it is difficult to fault. Every one of us who have spent our careers in education harbors a similar sentiment, and just the thought of such a system is exciting to think about.

The report itself is not shy about putting forth the paradigm of reform as the basis for advancing the cause of education: the subtitle of the report is *The Imperative for Educational Reform*. In the spirit of declaring the system broken, the authors of the report list thirteen fairly damning criticisms of the system (ten of them based on test scores) and then famously declare that as a result, "If an unfriendly foreign power had attempted to impose on America the mediocre educational performance that exists today, we might well have viewed it as an act of war."[4]

Thus, *reform* is the term that is now and for some time has been applied by those who declared our schools broken and in need of repair. The choice of that term has certainly served to emphasize the degree of brokenness in the system, as *reform* is not a tolerant term.

When something is in need of reform it is generally because of the notion that something bordering on evil or pernicious needs to be fundamentally changed. Reform schools of yesteryear were essentially penal institutions for unruly teenagers. Financial institutions were declared to be in need of reform after they were deemed to be culpable for much of the economic meltdown in 2008 and 2009.

The Reformation itself declared that the prevailing religious institution was itself fundamentally flawed and incapable of meeting the promise of religious salvation.

A Nation at Risk was motivated by the idea that schools were failing to produce students capable of serving in a competitive workforce and offered a series of findings that set forth the case for just how badly schooling was broken and in need of wholesale repair.[5] The findings were in four categories: the content that was being taught, the manner in which time was being spent, our low expectations for students, and the quality of our teaching force. Each has been extensively commented on (and extensively criticized) and has directly influenced the state of education as it stands today.

The recommendations that resulted from the findings were in the areas of content, standards and expectations, additional time for learning, additional support for teachers, and for leadership and fiscal support. All were given in the sprit of the then current system being broken and in need of repair.

One of the recommendations in the content area for teaching English is as follows (similar statements are included for other content areas):

> The teaching of English in high school should equip graduates to: (a) comprehend, interpret, evaluate, and use what they read; (b) write well-organized, effective papers; (c) listen effectively and discuss ideas intelligently; and (d) know our literary heritage and how it enhances imagination and ethical understanding, and how it relates to the customs, ideas, and values of today's life and culture. [6]

Every state has written something similar into their own standards for education, and while it is true that multiple definitions exist for things like "literary heritage" and "values of today's life and culture," states for the most part seem to have found interpretations regarding these outcomes that work for them.

What should be clear is that the call for educational standards that defined the basis for an education now exists in all fifty states. The impact of this recommendation has been significant.

Accompanying the recommendation for higher expectations was one that recommended standardized testing as the measure for whether or not students were meeting those expectations (standardized testing will be discussed at length in a later chapter). The recommendation is pretty clear: "Standardized tests of achievement (not to be confused with aptitude tests) should be administered at major transition points from one level of schooling to another and particularly from high school to college or work." [7]

As with the standards, every single state now requires a standardized testing program of its students at a majority of grades as the measure of its educational success. Again, this recommendation is now a predominant part of the educational landscape.

Now, consider another recommendation that had to do with the amount of time it would take for students to learn and demonstrate a much higher level of learning. The recommendation around time specifically states, "School districts and State legislatures should strongly consider 7-hour school days, as well as a 200- to 220-day school year," as well as points out that for students who struggle historically even more time may be needed. [8]

An additional recommendation in the teaching category then suggests that in order for all this to happen teachers will need to work on an eleven-month contract (as opposed to the more typical ten-month contract) and that they will need to be justly compensated for the additional work. [9]

In other words, the commission that created the report said that in order to fix the problems as identified that students would need to learn and do more than ever before, that it would take more time in class and more school days during the school year to do that, and that teachers would need to increase their ability to deliver on that promise and should be compensated for their increased workload. If all that happens, so the report strongly implies, then perhaps we might move the entire system closer to achieving the country's educational goals.

Thirty years have now passed since the report was issued, and one can argue that things have, to some degree improved. Certainly we pay attention to historically underserved populations like never before, and we have seen some upticks in terms of broad achievement measures and, most recently, in graduation rates.[10] But to say that the quality of education in America has surged would be a gross overstatement.[11]

One of the reasons may have something to do with the fact that while we now have standards and standardized tests we are still attempting to squeeze higher achievement out of students and teachers in the same 180-day calendar and ten-month teacher contracts that existed at the time of *A Nation at Risk* and that continue to this day.

Consider that the five sets of recommendations in *A Nation at Risk* actually fall into two broad categories. In one category we have the things that can be used to guide student achievement: standards and tests in particular. In the other category we have the changes to the actual system that need to be made in order to create those results: more hours in the classroom with students led by better-trained, better-paid teachers, as well as adequate educational resources commensurate with the higher expectations.

What have so far been implemented are the guides, but not the systems per se. It seems as if we want all the good things in the report without thinking we have to pay for them.

What is interesting in this regard is what the report doesn't say: the report doesn't say a word about how best to do all these things—and a great many others—out in the real world. It certainly suggests they should be accomplished, but it leaves the manner in which that is to be done up to others. It doesn't suggest an order to things, or a priority in the event of scarce resources.

The title of the report said it perfectly: this thing called education is broken and it all needs to be fixed. It offered recommendations in a number of categories, some that were needed to guide the new educational world they were envisioning, and some that were needed as the base supports that would allow that to occur.

Once you convince someone that the entire system is broken it seems that categories such as "guidelines" and "systems" no longer much matter—they are all needed and anything has to be better than what we have, even though guidelines and systemic change are profoundly different things.

All of the recommendations in *A Nation at Risk* were offered in the spirit of *reform*, which impacts the way they will be received. If I only need to convince you that something needs to be *improved*, then we don't even have to agree that a problem existed in order to plan and implement the improvement. It would be akin to the software upgrades that are now a part of owning a computer: most of the time we average users have no idea what we're missing until an upgrade offers us a new set of features that all of a sudden we can't believe we ever lived without. We don't have to know a problem exists in order to offer an improvement.

If, however, I convince you that the system is fundamentally broken and needs to be reformed, then all of a sudden it all needs to be fixed. And since it all needs to be fixed and you have to start somewhere, each part of the solution appears to present itself as something capable of improving the situation on its own *even if no other part of the solution is ever implemented.*

In an environment that needs to be reformed, a strange transformation occurs, presenting even the lowliest of solutions as capable of a similar effect as the most dramatic. After all, we have to start somewhere; even a small bit of a good system has to be better than what went before.

The result in the case of education is that the guidelines in the form of standards and assessments were seen as capable of having a profound effect even without a major systemic change. In an environment that needed to be reformed, having standards and standardized assessments could be said to have a similar effect to adding a month to the school year—it was just a matter of doing something and awaiting good results. If you could only pick one thing, that is still a step in the right direction of fixing what ails education and you can, theoretically, with each implemented component, increase expectations.

A policymaker faced with any list of equally appearing recommendations is going to prioritize the recommendations the way any policymaker would: by price and political expediency. Indeed, the recommendations best suited to actually increase student achievement in the form of longer school days and a longer school year were the most difficult to implement from a fiscal and political perspective and remain to this day unimplemented. The recommendations that were the easiest, cheapest, most politically expedient, but were also the least likely to increase student achievement on their own, are now mainstays in education: standards and standardized tests.

The fallacy, of course, is that not all the recommendations had to do with actually improving the outcome, and if the only recommendations selected were explicitly *not* about improving outcomes, you cannot rationally expect the outcomes to change. Yet that very expectation is built in to the school accountability systems also imposed by policymakers.

The simple reality is that policymakers implemented a set of policies designed for one purpose and now expect those policies to transmogrify into something they are not. Wishing, however, has not made it so. [12]

The use of a reform paradigm to drive change in schools has a second set of effects that are just as important to explore as those at the policy level. These effects have to do with who gets to make the decisions regarding educational quality as well as the manner in which such decisions are to be made. The most profound changes have to do with what I'll call the "arbiter of quality" and the manner in which it has been removed from the classroom—at least reading and mathematics classrooms—to a very large degree.

The word *arbiter* is not an accidental choice—it invokes both a notion of authority but also a notion of negotiator. Both meanings apply.

It helps to see just how profound this change has been if you think of the two dimensions involved in making a quality determination: the focus of the decision and who gets to make it. Table 2.1 breaks the focus of a decision into those focused on an individual's specific assignment or job and those who are focused on the larger organization.

The gray area between these is rather large, but the point can still be made that most decisions fit mainly in one or the other. The roles listed in each column help to show the differences.

The table also identifies that the quality determination can be made such that "I" am the arbiter of quality in regard to the decisions that are to be made or if that responsibility lies with someone else and it is my job to comply. The definition for what qualifies as "quality" almost always is larger than any system, so identifying the arbiter isn't about who gets to *define* what quality looks like but where a quality determination is to be made. Is it my job to apply the definition, or someone else's to apply it for me?

The dimensions in making a quality determination involve the focus or target of the decision and the position from which the quality determination

	The decision is focused on my assignment	The decision is focused on the larger organization
I am the arbiter of quality	• Leader • Manager • Teacher • Mentor	• Contributor • Team player • Consultant/ advisor
Someone else is the arbiter of quality	• Employee • Learner • Annual evaluation time	• Follower • Responder • Reactor

Table 2.1. The Dimensions in a Quality Determination

is made. Virtually every person in an organization participates in multiple roles on a daily basis, with the majority of time spent in one of the four resulting quadrants.

It doesn't matter who you are in an organization: the CEO, an assembly-line worker, a teacher, or a school superintendent; at any point in a day you will find yourself operating somewhere among the various roles, often in multiple roles. What will differ between assignments is where you spend the bulk of your time in regard to the various roles.

Assembly-line workers will spend the bulk of the day in the lower boxes, where others determine the quality of their work. Even when an assembly-line worker is empowered to make the quality determination, it is against a fairly rigid set of criteria, and the most important quality determination is often at the assembly-line or plant level.

CEOs will spend most of their time in the upper-left box, where it is their job to be the arbiter of quality over an entire organization, but they, too, are an employee of a board somewhere, and they cannot ignore Wall Street or the expectations of industry analysts and so would have to function in the lower two boxes as well.

Teachers are interesting in this regard. Historically teachers functioned almost exclusively in the left two boxes, with the bulk of their time devoted to the upper left, where they served as the arbiters of quality for the bulk of their decisions. Their preservice training was all about that role, the mentoring and student-teaching that took place was about ensuring that they were ready to take on that role, and a tenured teacher was someone who had successfully fulfilled that role for some period of time.

Teachers were certainly also employees (lower left) and had to adhere to rules and regulations as well as make sure they were paying attention to the established curriculum and working within the constraints of available textbooks and materials (lower right), but the bulk of their time was spent in a classroom with their students where they served as the arbiter of quality work—which is the very thing they were trained to do.

It wasn't that they could just not care about contributing to the organization (upper right), but the organization for them played a somewhat different role than a business: the organization was there to support them in doing their jobs; they were not employees working to ensure that the organization made a profit. They were teachers looking to lead their students to quality.

A Nation at Risk offered the possibility that the structure of teaching in this regard needed to be called into question. To be fair, education had remained largely unchanged during the lives of every living generation at the time, and any reasonable human being would likely have agreed that it was time for a set of improvements to be implemented. Education certainly needed be more inclusive, more creative, more about what the current generation of students really needs in order to have a solid foundation for future success.

The report offered policymakers a number of options by which to do this. The selection of which options to put in place, however, stood to either empower teachers—with professional salaries, more time to accomplish more learning with their students, and the assurance of proper materials and resources—or to impose a heavy-handed accountability system that presumed the problems were the fault of those same teachers. The options weren't presented in those terms, but in hindsight both were certainly a part of the mix.

The *At Risk* committee offered their solution for a fix that viewed the solution holistically: empower and professionalize teaching, provide far better guidelines than existed previously, resource the thing properly, and ensure that the system is run by talented leaders who have the tools they need to support the process. But because *reform* was the umbrella under which the task was to be accomplished, it created an irony of sorts: the suggestion was made to empower teachers, but those same teachers were also pilloried in the report as not being up to snuff and for coming from a tradition of teacher prep that was not academically what many might hope for a teacher. [13]

In that regard the report ran counter to itself and created a bit of a cart-and-horse problem: do you create those empowerments and look forward to the improvements you believe are needed, driven through higher salaries and the like, or do you punish those you see as responsible for the mess and punt the problem of actually improving the teaching force down the road?

Policymakers have, since that moment, been content to focus on punishment and continue to punt their support for professionalizing the teaching force to some future generation. As part of that punishment teachers were subsequently removed—in the subjects of reading and math—as the arbiters of quality. Rather than attempt to raise the teaching force called for in the report as a key component in the process, it was if policymakers decided that doing so just wasn't possible and thus needed to come up with a way to make mediocre teachers and schools toe the line.

It was as if someone at some point in the process decided that schools and teachers already had been given a sufficient amount of time and resources with which to do the job and were squandering it, making for the easy answer that teachers and schools just needed to work harder.

Since that point *test-based accountability* has been the repeated response to the perceived problem with the teaching force and is the direct outcome of the attitude that teachers are largely to blame for the need to even have education reform. Test-based accountability—which will be discussed at length in additional chapters—is the overly simple idea that the quality of everything that happens in a reading or a mathematics classroom or even an entire school can be summed up in a standardized test score.

It should suffice for now to point out just one example of the fallacious thinking in that idea: standardized tests are designed to allow researchers to understand how populations compare to each other, but they are absolutely silent as to *why* one population or student ranks ahead of or behind another. Any understanding of the *why* must be accomplished outside of the test itself, meaning that any statement regarding quality will have to occur independent of the test score. To presume otherwise is to ask the test to operate outside and beyond its design, which would be exactly like asking a stethoscope to do the work of a dental drill. It really is that inconceivable.

From a cynical perspective, however, policymakers weren't going to make an additional investment in the professionalization of teaching, since that would mean they risked being perceived as irresponsible for allowing those who created the mess to go unchecked. The best way for them to feel that they were doing their jobs under such a condition was to move the quality determination in the most fundamental content areas outside the teaching profession, and then they just happened to have selected an instrument designed for another purpose entirely.

In the systems that existed prereform what was valued was the power of the teacher to guide and direct student achievement in deeply personal and meaningful ways, making the teacher the central driver behind the educational formula. A primary role of teaching was to learn to make that quality determination, and while it was clear—as the evidence in *A Nation at Risk* showed—that we needed to do a better job in a whole variety of areas, removing teachers from this role is not among the recommendations.

The committee, however, established *reform* as the best means by which to motivate the changes, which in turn declared it all broken, which in turn allowed policymakers far more leeway in their approach to implementation than might have been intended.

Had the teaching force not been labeled as broken, removing teachers as the arbiter of quality may not have been seen as necessary, and it may have been much more politically acceptable to professionalize it, but that was not the case: it was declared broken, leaving policymakers with the choice to professionalize what was identified as a big part of the problem or punish it.

Policymakers had no choice but to act, but the mantra of reform left them free to treat the competing ideas of punishment of a bad system or the professionalization of the teaching force as equals, leaving political expediency and cost as the main criteria. Punishment wins that one hands down, and continues to do so until the present.

The declaration that education was in need of reform enabled a set of policies that effectively removed teachers as the arbiters of quality in reading and math, placing those decisions in the hands of standardized test scores. That creates a profoundly different role for a teacher to play in the educational formula than they have historically. The definition of quality has always been larger than a single classroom, but teachers have for as long as anyone can remember (prior to reform) served as the primary decision maker for quality determination.

Now that that role is elsewhere, it changes the nature of teaching: the job is to help students succeed against a definition very different than what most think of when they select education as a career. The teacher's role has been relocated to the lower half of the table (2.1 above) where the arbiter of quality is elsewhere.

The trend that began when it was declared that success was now in a standardized test score continues to pick up speed. Test scores have become a major component of both teacher and principal evaluations, and the federal government has placed stipulations to that effect on several of the funding sources they provide, requiring states to promise to hold teachers' feet to the fire or risk that funding. Nowhere is there any talk of the increased professionalization of teaching that the document that started the reform movement insisted should be considered as a part of the overall package.

I would be remiss not to point out what should have been an obvious question when the reform movement got underway: Was the problem the reformers wanted to address one of access for all to what good teachers and schools were able to offer, or a problem with what even the limited population of the best-served students were encountering?

If it was the latter, if no students were being well served, then positioning the arbiter of quality outside the classroom may have been justified, since even well-served students would be seen falling short. If it was the former, and the issue was one of access to quality schooling and that level of quality was in existence in at least some places, then the arbiter-of-quality problem wasn't the issue, and we would have been wise to focus on extending access instead.

Note that in the criteria that were listed justifying that the nation was indeed at risk virtually every indicator had to do with averages or subsections of the population, meaning that their own data failed to identify whether the issue was one of access or a fundamentally flawed system that all needed to be tossed aside and "reformed."[14] That leaves the report vulnerable to the criticism that concluding that the entire system is broken stems from something other than the data, because their data can only suggest that some in the system are achieving at a lower level than others. The rest is conjecture.

The reform paradigm—because it insisted it was all broken—allowed for the answer to be both access *and* quality: teachers weren't delivering on the promise of education, and even if they came close their focus was limited to certain segments of the population in a manner that is not scalable. It opened the possibility that all the answers may need to come from outside education. It didn't preclude the notion that what needed to be done was to take examples from teachers who were experiencing the greatest amount of success with the widest range of students and extend those findings to the whole of education, but it allowed for even that approach to be questioned.

The result is that teaching—especially teaching reading and mathematics—is eking ever closer to a homogenized approach, one that removes anything that stands in the way of a higher test score. From a policy perspective this is perfectly acceptable: teaching needs to be reformed and reprofessionalized, but lacking the resources to do that, then the idea is to standardize as much as is humanly possible to at least ensure a consistent result in spite of bad teachers.

The insistence needs to be upon a standardized outcome, based on test scores, and teachers should spend their time making sure that their students can pass those tests.

The idea is to push teachers as far away as possible from the quality determination, since the last time it was entrusted to them someone had to step in and reform the system they messed up. (It may sound like I'm practicing a bit of hyperbole here, but a quick read of the popular press regarding the teaching profession suggests that I'm not far off.)

Herein lies the irony in all this: our teachers—the very people most capable of carrying out the mission of educating our students, most of whom entered the profession with the idea of working hard to be good arbiters of quality when it comes to their decisions regarding students, and were expecting and looking forward to doing just that—are now asked to work against type.

Teachers find themselves faced with an environment where the arbiter of quality is external to the classroom and to them in the form of an "objective" standardized test that in turn, with the advent of school-based accountability to those test scores, means that the two greatest prizes to be sought by teachers are a rise in test scores and the subsequent survival of the school as a unit.

I'm not going to dwell too much on the point here, but jobs that have very little control over the quality determination and whose individual efforts are seen primarily through a lens in which the employee is a cog in a wheel are in factories on assembly lines. I am in no way disparaging what happens in factories—in fact, a great many modern factory workers make a great deal more than teachers and require as extensive a set of skills to do their job—but instead I am suggesting that when it comes to teaching and learning an assembly line full of processes that must be repeated over and over again is an inappropriate and wrong-headed model for teaching.

The reform paradigm removes teachers as the primary arbiter of quality and then redefines educational quality into something almost unrecognizable to those who teach. Such a paradigm certainly came into being as a result of a number of arguments people found compelling, and then as with any shift it enabled some things while placing limits on others.

Most notably when it comes to teachers, it allowed for policymakers faced with the apparent chance to truly professionalize teaching in a manner that was declared as necessary if the system was going to be improved to actually choose something else entirely.

With a little hindsight, we are now in an excellent position to understand the consequences of having chosen reform as the major metaphor for improving our schools. The most serious of these consequences is that we now task teachers to educate all of our students to a very high level and then ask them to accomplish that in an environment where their power to make decisions is profoundly limited, and the quality of those decisions is measured externally to the classroom using instruments that have little to do with quality instruction.

The additional irony is that when students fail to meet whatever expectations we might have, the continued tendency is to blame teachers—the very people whose value in the system and authority to make decisions is now considerably less than it was. A good deal of the authority teachers once had has now been placed outside classrooms, so it should make sense that if educational shortcomings remain the responsibility for them then it should be seen at the very least as a shared issue that includes those broader systemic pieces.

Instead, the system itself isn't questioned. Rather, teachers are. The very clear assumption in policy after policy requiring that teacher accountability be tied to the test scores of their students is that the system as it is is fine, and that the problem is that teachers need to try harder, albeit in an environment where their influence and power is greatly reduced and the new paradigms for their work are foreign to and inappropriate for the profession.

Returning teachers to a professionalized role is imperative if we are to see the surge in achievement that every policymaker desires.

Remember that policymakers had a very specific set of recommendations from *A Nation at Risk*—an extended school day and an extended school year, and the professionalization of the teaching force—that offered a real chance at increasing achievement, but had they implemented any of them it could have been suggested that teachers up to that point were in fact doing their jobs and needed additional time and resources if more was going to be accomplished.

Implementing those recommendations could have been seen as a pat on the back to the teaching force that they were doing the best they could with what they had and that if we desired something different they required something more.

Instead, the reform paradigm allows policymakers to suggest that teachers were not in fact doing their jobs, and therefore more could be accomplished if the existing resources were better used. Had policymakers opted for the recommendations of extended time, an extended school year, and the professionalization of the teaching force, that may have empowered teachers. What a different educational landscape might have awaited us. But somehow the decision was made to work from a position in which it was all broken, making it possible to reject any recommendation that implied teachers were doing anything close to okay.

This, in turn, opened both the economic and the intellectual coffers of education to a host of outsiders for whom access was previously denied. It started a landslide in terms of educational leaders suddenly finding they reported to a governor or mayor rather than an elected or appointed board. Consider that a significant number of leading educational positions in this country are now filled with former military and business leaders with zero educational background, and that the only educational universe they can possibly know is one that consists of a flawed set of educational metrics.

In addition, the number of educational organizations inside the D.C. beltway has since mushroomed, filled with staffers that have never taught a child and yet are set up as experts in all things related to education. While some of these groups are clearly supportive of the teaching process, the majority seem just as focused on raising funds to keep themselves afloat and attach themselves to whatever the latest initiative that policymakers and funders believe to be the next big thing, but rarely is the experience in a classroom enhanced as a result.

These groups, too, have commercial reasons to keep the status quo in place, since their own livelihood depends on it. They have institutionalized themselves around various parts and pieces of the reform paradigm, and they risk their institutional lives should the system move in a manner for which they aren't prepared. The bottom line of the reform paradigm is that educational novices that lack a motive to actually learn or change now run a significant part of education. This further allows for the assumption that the decisions of these educational novices are capable of transforming the educational enterprise and that any lack of transformation is the fault of teachers not trying hard enough. It doesn't allow for the consideration that policies made in the name of reform might be dead wrong, or that the people trying to steer the ship are operating from a bad set of assumptions or a very limited understanding of what it takes to educate a child.

That leaves us at a very odd point.

Absent the reform paradigm, policymakers still might have made the same decisions, but here some thirty years later they would not have been able to blame teachers as the primary source for the fact that achievement didn't rise as expected.

They would have had to acknowledge that however useful standards and standardized tests were for their intended purposes they were insufficient on their own for truly advancing student achievement. And if they had made different decisions these would be viewable through a more objective lens for their value and efficacy. Teachers in any of these scenarios may well be found to be a part of the problem, but in a world driven by something other than reform they might be seen as the key to the solution and not as an unfortunate but necessary part to the system that needs to be controlled so they can't mess things up again.

The use of the reform paradigm isn't likely to see its demise for the foreseeable future. Categorizing education as a thing that is fundamentally broken offers a very convenient position from which to make policy decisions, because anything and everything counts as an improvement. Policymakers need not do their homework as to what works or how best to accomplish the task, but they can claim political successes based on change that really is just change for the sake of change.

It allows them to tackle the problem piecemeal, should resources become available, but not to have to ask the tough questions about what a complete education of the type our students deserve might actually consist of.

NOTES

1. Richard Rorty, *Contingency, Irony, and Solidarity* (Cambridge: Cambridge University Press, 1989), 9.

2. Rorty, *Contingency, Irony, and Solidarity*, 3–4.

3. Richard Gardner, chair, *A Nation at Risk: The Imperative for Educational Reform* (Washington, DC: The National Commission on Excellence in Education, 1983), iv.

4. Gardner, *A Nation at Risk*, 5.

5. Gardner, *A Nation at Risk*, 6–7.

6. Gardner, *A Nation at Risk*, 25.

7. Gardner, *A Nation at Risk*, 28.

8. Gardner, *A Nation at Risk*, 29.

9. Gardner, *A Nation at Risk*, 31.

10. Robert Stillwell and Jennifer Sable, *Public School Graduates and Dropouts from the Common Core of Data: School Year 2009–10: First Look (Provisional Data)* (Washington, DC: U.S. Department of Education: National Center for Education Statistics, 2013), 4.

11. One of the more compelling arguments regarding the lack of a surge can be made by looking at scores for the National Assessment of Educational Progress (NAEP). Since 1992 scores in key content areas have ticked upward, but nothing resembling a move commensurate with the dollars invested in the name of reform is to be seen. By any measure, the return on the investment has to be seen as less than stellar. NAEP results can be accessed at http://nces.ed.gov/nationsreportcard/.

12. There were, of course, additional recommendations that were acted on, for example, in the area of leadership training, and others that were not, such as making teacher salaries commensurate with other professional groups. What is interesting for the argument here is that the pattern seems to hold: the things that were politically expedient but had little to do with increasing actual achievement were considered or implemented, while those that were expensive but stood the best chance of creating such an increase were not.

13. Gardner, *A Nation at Risk*, 22.

14. Gardner, *A Nation at Risk*, 8–9.

Chapter Three

The Trouble with *Rigor*

At a conference several years ago that included lots of laypeople with a deep interest in education and a few from within the educational community, a panel member at one of the plenary sessions spoke to the need for "increased rigor in education."

He wasn't making up the phrase or using it in a manner that anyone close to education hadn't heard a thousand times before, but a fellow who identified himself as an engineer stood and questioned the use of the term, pointing out that *rigor* has to do with precision and exactness, such as that necessary to prove a particular scientific theory or the degree of precision required in a good set of plans for a bridge or skyscraper.

When I looked up the term later, I noticed that the only definition that might relate to education (but not an education I would choose to participate in) represents the idea of "unyielding harshness," as in "the rigors of winter."

It is, as well, the root of good old *rigor mortis*, which is hardly a proper metaphor for a dynamic education. How strange that we would have chosen a term and assigned it a meaning that frankly doesn't exist. There are consequences for having done that. It's not that it can't come to mean something new, but rather, absent a more formal definition, the term is free to function with less meaning than it deserves.

The fact that it lacks any degree of precision (i.e., rigor) means that we are free to use the term as if it has real meaning, without ever having to truly describe what that meaning is. It may sound good when used, but it also may not mean much.

And yet, *rigor* is the primary adjective used by reformers and adopted by a great many others to describe what education should be. That is a strange choice and one that really is problematic. *Rigor* is now used as a beard of sorts that masks all sorts of irreconcilabilities that cannot possibly coexist in a healthy system. The future of education is in trouble if we allow that sort of nonsense to continue.

Those who are termed reformers apply the term *rigorous* to standards, assessments, and to the educational enterprise as a whole as an adjudicating statement by which to judge the quality of each. In doing so they are moving well beyond any denotative meanings.

When I think of what I desire for my own children in terms of an education, lots of words come to mind: *rich, meaningful, dynamic, challenging,* and *deep,* to name just a few. The surprising thing is that those who now use the term *rigor* as an educational adjective seem to be referencing some or all of those meanings, even though they have virtually nothing in common with the historical meanings in terms of both meaning and tone ("unyielding harshness" and "dynamic education," for example, aren't even in the same ballpark).

This new and somewhat puzzling usage, then, cannot help but invoke a sort of schizophrenia, meaning one thing to those who support educational reform and quite another to those who read that one of the goals of education reform is to make education a rigorous enterprise.

"But so what?" one might say. And indeed, this may look like I'm just arguing over semantics. After all, it is characteristic of the English language to borrow and adapt terms and words from others (*rigor* has Latin roots, as do a great many of the terms we use on a daily basis), and the meanings attached to words change over time with use, which is exactly what, it could be argued, seems to be happening here.

The fact that the historical meaning and decidedly severe tone morphed into what is clearly a positive distant cousin still just represents the process of language adapting in the context of use. So the argument continues, an Internet search on *rigor* and *education* results in millions of hits, meaning that there is no going back.

Consider how far the new meanings have evolved. In a popular education book by Barbara Blackburn actually titled *Rigor Is Not a Four-Letter Word,* the following definition is offered:

> Rigor is creating an environment in which each student is expected to learn at high levels, each student is supported so he or she can learn at high levels, and each student demonstrates learning at high levels. [1]

Now the complete definition from Merriam Webster:

Rigor

1. a (1): harsh inflexibility in opinion, temper, or judgment: severity (2): the quality of being unyielding or inflexible: strictness (3): severity of life: austerity b: an act or instance of strictness, severity, or cruelty
2. a tremor caused by a chill
3. a condition that makes life difficult, challenging, or uncomfortable; especially: extremity of cold
4. strict precision: exactness <logical rigor>
5. a obsolete: rigidity, stiffness b: rigidness or torpor of organs or tissue that prevents response to stimuli c: rigor mortis[2]

Only in the part of the denotative dictionary definition regarding a *challenging condition* do we find anything even remotely related to the definition offered by Blackburn, but notice that the word *challenging* is wedged between *difficult* and *uncomfortable*, and the example clarifies the tone of the term: "especially extremity of cold."

A complete examination of how and when *rigor* was first used to describe a desirable educational state is beyond this book, but at various points I'll offer a few semi-informed opinions. Regardless, what is clear is a great many are now using the term in a manner completely removed from its denotative meaning.

Eventually, the dictionary meaning may adjust and add a new meaning regarding a desired state in education, but in the meantime the invented use of the word allows for consensus regarding the value of the term as a term, while also allowing for as many different meanings as there are users to offer one. Thus, you and I may agree completely that education should be a *rigorous* enterprise, and yet if we delved deeper we will likely have very different ideas for what that means.

If so, we may well be guilty of agreeing at a semantic level—at the level at which we utter the word—but not at a level where meaning occurs. That is a game of semantics that must be explored, because we may not be agreeing at all.

The danger of such imprecision lies with the fact that *rigor* is now the adjudicating factor for whether or not something can be accepted into the educational milieu. Educational standards are acceptable if and only if they are rigorous. The assessments that accompany them are designed to be rigorous. A rigorous education is a good education.

Because of the lack of real definition for its current use, uttering *rigor* in fact references almost nothing, simply because it can mean anything. It risks becoming a synonym for *good* without anyone having to explain what *good* really means, since *rigor* is the point. When an explanation of one's usage of *rigor* is forthcoming, the fact that the usage is new and in the process of changing the language leaves the speaker free to add to it whatever meanings are helpful to make their point.

In saying this, I want to be clear that this is precisely how language morphs and evolves over time. If you look at the histories of words in the *Oxford English Dictionary* you see a record of a term's usage and how the term has worked its way into present usage. The application of the term *rigor* is so pervasive in education at present that—as I hinted at above—I cannot help but imagine that future editions of the OED will offer an example or two related to education.

The new definitions and their various applications are numerous. Sometimes a desire for rigorous tests refers to the desire for higher test scores and sometimes for tougher tests. The call for rigorous standards in some states is interpreted with a level of rigidity such that if it isn't testable on a multiple-choice exam then it shouldn't be taught and in others as standards that offer something to aspire to and thus aren't testable at all. Blackburn's definition quoted above is one of hundreds that are attempting to invoke some state of education that the educational enterprise needs to attempt to produce.

Thus the term *rigor* means, in order of the above examples, *higher, tougher, precise, something to aspire toward,* and for Blackburn's definition, an esoteric sense for how the system should be balanced. This, by the way, is just a sprinkling of what is out there. Which is exactly the point. Since no single or unifying definition currently exists for the term's application to education, then to some degree all the new and disparate meanings offer a similar level of validity. That means that as a term it is severely lacking in any sort of practical, adjudicating power. If I want something to be rigorous, because being rigorous is a good thing, odds are I can find among the many competing definitions one that fits, and thereby attach the term to the thing and declare it so. Or I can come up with my own definition, and if it seems compelling, add it to the mix.

I can then share in the educational reform community's use of the term, making me a part of that community and offering my agreement that things should be rigorous, without ever completely revealing what that means.

Hidden beneath the educational community's use of such a term is the fact that serious incompatibilities exist between definitions, but the level of power in the term *rigor* allows for an implicit agreement to substitute for and even displace those deeper meanings. Using powerful terms such as *rigor* to cover up what would otherwise be incompatible positions in this manner is an old rhetorical trick, and we shouldn't be surprised in this case by its use, however inadvertent it may be.

Such powerful terms operate as a normal part of daily life: *democracy, conservatism,* and *liberalism,* for example, are three such terms that have achieved that sort of power in their current incantations: lots of people now circle their wagons around one or more of them and defend them or pillory them quite vehemently, and yet even the popular press greatly distorts the historical tradition and denotative meaning of each. Like *rigor*, the point isn't to get to the level of meaning but to create consensus around the term itself.

Terms that develop power such that the focus is on the level of the utterance and not on the underlying meaning allow for incompatibilities to coexist and remain unresolved, which in very complex situations dismisses the need to actually understand something, because understanding diminishes the power of the term. Understanding, for example, that *liberalism* and *conservatism* are anything but the polar opposites represented by pundits who make their careers dithering about such things diminishes the power of the terms and makes each more accessible to the other side for conversation and discussion. That accessibility would promote something other than punditry and as such would force a reasonable conversation, which threatens those pundits' careers.

Whether the unwillingness to ferret out a powerful term's various meanings occurs out of laziness when someone isn't willing to delve into and understand a complex situation or the desire to join a community by adopting their language, the result is the same: it allows for people to reach consensus at the level at which a word is uttered and feel as if something has been accomplished, while in point of fact nothing may have been resolved.

The severely uncritical use of *rigor* in education has gathered a huge community of users who would insist it has the power to serve as an adjudicating force, but in truth it has done very little other than to unify those who support educational reform.

In saying this I don't intend to ascribe motive. I merely mean to point out what has happened and suggest that it is harming the educational enterprise. As I have said, underlying all these things that are now deemed rigorous are incompatibilities being forced to coexist in a manner that cannot help but damage the educational system.

Consider, for example, that standardized tests require only a small sliver of content in order to show the distribution of students in a content area, so placing accountability on that small sliver of content risks reducing the curriculum to that content. However, because the content is derived from standards that are deemed rigorous, and the passing score on the test is said to be rigorous, a policymaker can declare the whole system that reduces teaching to a limited number of those standards to be rigorous and therefore good, without any indication of what any of that actually means.

Or, consider that we now hold teachers accountable for success in that constrained system to the point that we threaten to fire them if they can't succeed in it, and then limit their ability to make the choices that may be the right ones for students, all in the name of rigor. An accountability system that can result in the dismissal of "bad" teachers can be declared rigorous, and because of the rigor in the system teachers should be able to thrive.

Then, of course, there are all the additional definitions, some that refer to the level of challenge in the material, some to the sorts of things that Blackburn talks about, some use it to refer to the complexity of reading text, and still others to talk about the degree of difficulty in a test or a test score. It is quite literally in that sense a grammatically correct thing to suggest that every student in this country deserves a rigorous education that involves rigorous content taught in a rigorous manner such that they can pass a rigorous test with a rigorous passing score such that students can be prepared for the rigors ahead, even though the underlying realities may be in direct conflict with each other.

Again, the useful limit of the term is to identify users of it as part of the same group, because in reality it forces a whole bunch of incompatibilities to try to get along and, since they are all rigorous, they are blind to the fact that they cannot.

Education will always be dominated by powerful terms. In fact, one of the things that define a field of study, a profession, or an organization is the language that is unique to that field of study, profession, or organization, and each of them develop terms that occupy various points in the hierarchy, with some of them eventually rising to the top as those that define the field. At present, educational reformers unify themselves around terms such as *standards*, *rigor*, *reform*, and others.

As a simple example of how important language is to a field, think back to the first few days on a job and how much of the time was consumed with trying to learn what all the acronyms meant as well as the unique names for all sorts of things, and how quickly those that were deemed as central to the organization became a part of your own vocabulary. Professions such as law and medicine have hugely sophisticated vocabulary systems, and part of what comprises each field of study will be the leading terms used by its practitioners.

A Nation at Risk, by the way, is a good candidate for the guilty party for having introduced the term *rigor* into the educational reform vernacular. The report used the term *rigorous* five times to reference academic standards and examinations, to describe the type of effort that should be required from students, the standards again, and the textbooks and materials students require.[3]

We should not be surprised that educational reformers are attempting to establish a vocabulary to represent their place in the educational enterprise, but that doesn't mean we shouldn't explore what is revealed by those selections, and how (and if) they serve to gloss over real incompatibilities.

It is certainly common for a new and emerging field—and education reform in 1983 was very much an emerging field—to look at a field of study, a profession, or an organization that holds a level of respect with which the new field wishes to be aligned and adjust a vocabulary to align it with theirs. This can occur subconsciously—think about kids (the schoolyard is an organization, to be sure) adopting the language of the cool kids at school and much to their parents' and grammar teachers' chagrin bringing it home with them—but it can also occur quite subconsciously.

Consider the "dot-com" phase of the late 1990s when companies that added ".com" to their names suddenly found their market valuation soaring no matter that all that existed was an idea, or politicians that attempt to associate themselves with terms focus groups have identified as having a positive connotation and their opponent with terms deemed to be negative.

It is in this vein that I think it fairly easy to see one way in which the term *rigor* might have come to be used in educational circles—and certainly in *A Nation at Risk*. Educational research and classroom practice as of thirty or so years ago were perceived to be miles apart. (I won't argue here whether that was or was not the case. I am only concerned here with the perception, and with the subsequent and substantial federal investment in projects such as the What Works Clearinghouse that was set up to showcase quality research that educators can count on as they make decisions, or asking the Regional Educational Laboratories to focus on randomized controlled trials for their studies, that I think was and to some degree continues to be very real.)

Good research was seen as an important part of a complete educational package, and the standard for good research is the degree of rigor in it following historical denotations: Was it indeed thorough, accurate, and exhaustive? If it was, then it should be used to influence and guide change in schools.

At the time the current reform movement was just underway, research was seen as a good thing and something schools had failed to act on to a proper degree, but schools, as evidenced by the perceived need to reform them, were viewed negatively. In what represented a huge, etymological leap the sense seems to have been that if good research is rigorous, then a good education could and should be rigorous as well.

Forget that the tortured analogy fails at so many levels: research is always by definition finite and limited in its scope—especially rigorous research—while schools and the process of education are almost infinite in their variety and their needs. In addition, rigorous research is *thorough*, *exhaustive*, and *accurate*—terms that have distant corollaries in education such as *sufficient*, *challenging*, and *meaningful*, but that hardly mean the same thing.

Regardless of whether or not research was the land bridge by which *rigor* became associated with *reform*, certainly the notion that a rigorous education was a good thing didn't happen overnight. As always happens when a term takes on new meanings, it was tried out and seemed to work and then someone else tried it and then someone influential used it and the process was off and running. Eventually, it achieved a level of power in its use that far outweighed whatever meanings were being ascribed, and it became vogue to use it, however and whenever possible.

Again, a simple Internet search will pull up millions of incidents of such use, and a plethora of meanings.

But thirty years in the history of a term is nothing, especially for one of Latinate origin that goes back some two thousand years. *Rigor* remains a nascent, immature term in regard to its participation in education, and as such its real value comes from invoking it whenever possible regardless of the meaning intended. Until that meaning solidifies to some degree we would do well to apply the historical meaning of the term to our present usage of it and certainly to find some other criteria for judging the quality of education—criteria that actually mean something and that don't mask the incompatibilities in so important a system.

These incompatibilities are the reason the term has been given a place in this book: as long as we can use terms any old way we want we won't have to address the incompatibilities that are harming the system. A little adherence to the historical definition of the seminal terms in what we refer to as educational reform stands a reasonable chance of laying bare the incompatibilities so that we can do something about them.

NOTES

1. Barbara Blackburn, *Rigor Is Not a Four-Letter Word* (Larchmont, NY: Eye on Education, 2008), 16.

2. I use Merriam Webster because it comes up first on an Internet search for online dictionaries and for no other reason. However, it has become something of a ritual for me to open any dictionary I come across and search for the term *rigor*. I have yet to find anything that differs much from what Merriam Webster offers.

3. Richard Gardner et al., *A Nation at Risk: The Imperative for Education Reform* (Washington, DC: The National Commission on Excellence in Education, 1983), 14–28.

Chapter Four

The Idea of Educational Standards

Another term that has been critical in the effort to improve schooling in this country is *standard*. Whereas *rigor* is a semantic offender that enables lots of incompatibilities to coexist, avoids resolution, and thereby risks damaging the educational enterprise, *standard* is a term that in practice actually gets in the way of what it purports to do.

Like *rigor*, it functions as a unifying term with almost universal agreement that a standards-based education is a good thing, but the form of our educational standards misses the intended mark. In fact, in its current incantation, a standards-based education misses the ability to produce a standards-based education by a good bit.

The International Organization for Standardization website defines a standard as "a document that provides requirements, specifications, guidelines or characteristics that can be used consistently to ensure that materials, products, processes and services are fit for their purpose." The American National Standards Institute website adds: "They may establish size or shape or capacity of a product, process or system. They can specify performance of products or personnel. They also can define terms so that there is no misunderstanding among those using the standard." These are two of the leading standards organizations in the world, so their definitions have some standing.

The standards they produce actually come in a variety of shapes and sizes. I have discovered any number of lists for the various types of standards that operate in government and industry and find that the following categories (these are my terms, by the way) capture the vast majority of them:

1. *Target Standards* operate as a goal, or as something to aspire to; for example, cars that average 50 miles to the gallon, or light bulbs that use 50 percent less energy than five years ago. Standards intended to

operate as a target are written as an expectation. They are generally put forward by those in a position of power who have no idea how the standard will be accomplished, and they offer very little in the way of detail regarding how to get it done, and while they are intended to require a real stretch to reach them they need to at least be perceived as rational. The point is to encourage creativity and innovation in a desirable direction.

2. *Conformity Standards* are detailed specifications designed to standard-ize a part of an industry; for example, the size of a gas nozzle, the shape of a plug, the dimensions on a roll of film, or the size of batter-ies. Some of these standards offer a definition of terms so that at the very least an industry can use a term meaningfully. Standards de-signed to standardize or define something offer a set of specifications that define the standard, and they are often exceedingly detailed. Such standards almost always come from inside an industry when the indus-try realizes that such standardization creates a needed efficiency that in turn frees resources to focus on other things.

3. *Imposed Standards* are those that a government agency determines are necessary as a protection for its citizens. Health and safety standards are obvious examples; for example, limits on power plant emissions, minimum safety regulations for mines, or permissible levels of chemi-cals in our food, but so, too, are standards imposed on banks to keep loan language simple and understandable. Building standards are in this category as well. Such standards most often represent thresholds established as a negotiation between scientists and researchers, indus-try, and government, and they almost always represent a compromise between competing interests. In addition, such standards are generally imposed from outside the industry, even though industry experts gen-erally have a seat at the table.

4. *Certification Standards* define a process an individual or an organiza-tion needs to follow in order to earn a recognition; for example, a software engineering certificate that shows the bearer knows how to ensure a consistent and predictable process or outcome, or a certifica-tion showing a person knows how to manage a project or product, or an accreditation for a university that makes their credits transferable to other similarly accredited schools. Such standards are generally disci-pline based and allow for an organization to elevate its own practices as it comes into compliance with the standards. It also allows for organizations to differentiate themselves from one another by the par-ticular industry standards each embraces and meets. These standards are generally met when an organization has completed a set of require-ments that earn the organization a certification from an accrediting source.

Table 4.1 summarizes and includes some additional information regarding each of these categories of standards. The point of the chart is to show that each category of standard has a purpose, is put in place from a variety of positions, can look very different, and can motivate very different sorts of behaviors through a variety of means.

	Purpose	Where does it generally come from?	What does the standard looks like?	What is the intended outcome?	What is the compliance question?	Consequence of non-compliance
Target Standard	Encourage in an intended direction	Outside the field, from a position of authority or influence	Specific target statement	Focus available resources towards meeting the standard	How does the actual result compare to the standard?	Missed reward
Conformity standard	Standardize or define a process, product, etc.	Inside the field, when efficiency will serve both the field and its consumers	Detailed specification	Standardize a component in an industry that allows the industry to innovate and compete elsewhere	Is the result in line with the specifications?	Missed commercial opportunities and industry efficiencies
Imposed Standards	Determine acceptable tolerances	Outside the field from a position with regulatory authority	Limits, tolerances, requirements	Compliance will result in a safer, healthier world in which to live	Upon inspection, were the tolerances met?	Penalties, sanctions
Certification standard	Identify the capability of an organization or individual	From an established discipline that exists in multiple fields (e.g., software engineering, project management)	A set of processes and activities to be accomplished	Organizations or individuals that complete the process will show evidence of a requisite set of skills and abilities	Did the submission meet the necessary criteria?	Inability to differentiate offerings, skill sets,

Table 4.1. Four Categories of Standards

However different each of the categories of standards is, they do have some very important things in common.

1. They are all *precise*. The intent of that precision differs widely, from setting a broad parameter that is obvious to anyone who sees it to specifications that offer a definition down to the most finite level of specification possible. The term *precise*, however, is not to be confused with the term *detailed*. Something can be precise and not detailed, it can be detailed and still lack precision, or it could be both detailed and precise. Precision has to do with being sharply defined, while a detail is a part of a larger thing. Just because something is detailed does not mean it can operate as one of the standards described above—a standard must first and foremost be *precise*.

2. The objective regarding any standard is *compliance*. Its primary point is to be met. Some categories of standards can be exceeded, but the standard is usually designed to identify single, not multiple points. Only in the target standard might someone partially meet it and receive credit for doing so, but even then it can only be expressed in terms of the standard and the degree to which the standard was missed or exceeded.

3. All measures are *direct*, and not via *proxies*. If the standard is that cars must run at 50 miles per gallon, then that is also the measure for compliance. If an industry standardizes a component, those specifications are the measurement criteria. If the government established an engineering specification for building codes, the building code is the measure. And since the standard must be measured directly, that measure must be applied *rigorously*![1]

Consider the manufacture of a car and how the various types of standards play out in that process. Clearly we have target standards for things such as gas mileage, conformity standards for the size of the gas nozzles at gas stations that will have to be accommodated, imposed standards in terms of emissions, and certification standards for the computer programmers, designers, engineers, and many of the labor groups that will assemble the car.

These things work together in the process of building the car that help keep costs down so that cars are reasonably affordable as well as safe and efficient, and it gives us confidence that they were properly built, won't fall apart the instant we drive off the lot, and that the nozzle at the gas station will fit.

For the sake of making standards easy to talk about, from this point forward I'll refer to standards that fit into the categories described thus far in this chapter as *fulfillment* standards. That term seems to offer a good sense regarding what such standards attempt to get us to do, and in a moment I will show how such statements differ from some other things also labeled as standards.

Fulfillment standards do not dictate the means by which they will be met. Even in the certification standard, which often defines a process and just as often involves a certification or licensure test of some sort, the manner in which required material is learned or presented as evidence is up to the individual or the institution seeking the certification. When it comes to conformity standards, the component could be manufactured one at a time by hand or mass-produced, so long as the standard is adhered to in an equally rigorous manner and the parts would be, in effect, interchangeable.

Thus the measures represented in a fulfillment standard do not define or dictate across an entire enterprise but offer limits, guidelines, and targets for certain parts of the enterprise.

Each type of fulfillment standard serves a decidedly different *rhetorical* function. I say *rhetorical* because each persuades activity in a very different manner. A target standard, for example, *compels* a hopefully infinite variety of behaviors in an effort to achieve the standard without commenting upon which behaviors are best.

A conformity standard tightly *constrains* a component in an industry in order to create efficiencies and free resources to focus elsewhere. An imposed standard places *limitations* and *thresholds* on what can be done and often how things can be done with sanctions for a failure to comply—many of which threaten the livelihood of a noncomplying institution.

And a certification standard stands as the meaning of the term *standard*, as in *standard bearer*, where it serves as an emblem of accomplishment that signals competence, discipline, and more.

Fulfillment standards have had a huge impact on society at large, and they affect every one of us every single day, from the air we breathe to the food we eat to the products we buy, the buildings we live in, and the manner in which the companies we work for operate. They improve the quality of things, make us safer, and make the manufacturing of products more efficient and cheaper. They enable innovation and help drive us toward larger societal goals.

The leap of standards from industry to education is not hard to imagine. At the time *A Nation at Risk* was written, the system that educated students was fragmented, produced some staggering discrepancies in terms of outcomes, and offered few efficiencies, particularly when it came to scaling best practices from one location to another. Publishing companies controlled much of the content that went into schools (in many cases because there was no one else to do it), and there were as many different delivery mechanisms as there were schools and districts.

Education was believed to be the engine by which we would drive the economies of the future and maintain our edge over the rest of the world, and since it was underperforming at great peril to that future it seemed a natural fit for what standards offer. After all, our educational system should aspire to be the best in the world, should seek to find and take advantage where efficiencies exist, and should establish benchmarks in terms of schooling outcomes. It most certainly should create certification programs for schools and students to show the value of what each had achieved.

In fact, a rich set of standards properly applied in an industry or field that suffered from a similar set of maladies had served as a way to reset poor performing systems or industries, oftentimes in a very short time frame and often with dramatic results. Standards for factory conditions, automobile efficiency, and various Internet protocols, for example, provided workers, customers, and users with a safer, better, and more efficient world in a relatively short period of time. It can easily be understood in that light that if educational improvement was the goal and time was of the essence, then a rich set of standards was just the thing.

Let's return to the standard for high schools offered in *A Nation at Risk* and referenced in an earlier chapter, since it represented an early attempt to bring the value of standards to education:

> The teaching of *English* in high school should equip graduates to: (a) comprehend, interpret, evaluate, and use what they read; (b) write well-organized, effective papers; (c) listen effectively and discuss ideas intelligently; and (d) know our literary heritage and how it enhances imagination and ethical understanding, and how it relates to the customs, ideas, and values of today's life and culture.

No matter how well the statement suggests what any rational human being would consider to be a reasonable list of things that we should expect from our high schools, when compared to a fulfillment standard the statement actually falls surprisingly short. It lacks any sort of *precision*; it doesn't seem to be about *compliance*, but rather a guide, or a set of objectives, or even a rubric for a successful high school, and finally, because it lacks precision any measure of success would have to be indirect and therefore would require a *proxy*.

I need to take a moment here to describe what is meant by a *proxy* and why I choose to use it in this context, since I will do so repeatedly from this point forward. A *proxy* generally references a deputy or individual that is authorized or empowered to stand in for another—a formal substitute, if you will. One of the meanings goes so far as to touch on the existence of a document that awards the authority to another, and it is this part of the meaning that makes sense when thinking about measurement.

Some things can be measured directly—such as a fulfillment standard—while others are very difficult to measure and require a roundabout approach. When those roundabout approaches take on the authority of a direct measure and we give them the same weight as the direct measure, we can say that the indirect measure has taken on proxy status, and we accept it just as we would the direct measure.

It is always important to know whether a metric is a direct measure or a proxy, because they need to be treated differently. If something is a direct measure, I can manage to the measure and the result is still in line with the goal. If something is a proxy and I manage to it, I risk a result that is well outside the goal. Knowing that a measure has proxy status lets me avoid making that mistake.

One hypothetical example should help make the point.[2] Let's say I wanted to measure the girth of the average American so that I can know the minimum specifications for airline seats, doorways, and chairs in waiting rooms, and that I wanted to do it state by state so as to understand regional differences. Let's also say that I drew a representative sample of Americans that I wanted to measure and then hired the field staff to spread out across the country and take the measurements of the tens of thousands of people that would be needed for such a study to be sufficiently precise so as to be useful.

What my hundreds or even thousands of data collectors would likely find is that knocking on a door and asking someone who doesn't know you if you can wrap a measuring tape around their widest parts is probably not going to be met with universal success. However, being smart people we could quickly seek out a proxy for the measures that are hard or (in this case) a little embarrassing to take.

Weight and height would provide an excellent proxy for the simple reason that they would provide an excellent correlation to the girth of Americans, and they would cut back dramatically on the number of potentially awkward encounters. It would then be up to the leaders of the study to measure the height, weight, and girth of only a small percentage of participants in the study until they were able to establish a correlation, and then extend those correlations to the rest of the population in the study for whom the only measures you had were height and weight.

What we would have done in that study is make weight and height a proxy for girth. But here is why we need to know that the vast majority of the measures we took represented a proxy: in each of those cases we failed to measure the thing that actually matters. That's okay, because we had a way of making an interpretive leap to what did matter. Absent that interpretive lens, the data are worthless in terms of the goal of the study.

Standardized tests are proxies for achievement in exactly the same way. A standardized test offers a rank ordering of students against a small piece of a domain that can stand in as a proxy for something far more difficult to measure or see: student achievement. From there, a researcher can apply an interpretive lens that allows them to view the rank ordering appropriately.

For example: How does my school's rank ordering compare to other school's rank orderings that once ranked as mine does now that has since improved their standing in dramatic fashion? The odds are that finding just such a school offers an opportunity to learn from them in an attempt to improve my own school's standing.

Consider the very different worlds that are created when I then attempt to manage to the proxy versus manage to the interpretation shown me through a proper interpretive lens: in the case of managing to the proxy of a test score I risk teaching to the test as a legitimate response. However, when I apply the proper interpretive lens, teaching to the test isn't even an option: the only option given that lens is to find those schools that are similar to mine who greatly improved their standing in legitimate ways and attempt to replicate what they did.

Proxies on their own are powerful devices for gathering data when direct measures are impossible, but they must never be confused with the direct measure, or they risk interpretations that are misleading at best, or just plain spurious at worse.

To return to the *At Risk* standard above, it is, at best, a list of some of the details that should be a part of a high school curriculum. It should be clear that the *At Risk* standard doesn't exactly fit any of the traditional definitions for what a standard is and should do. Is it a target standard intended to motivate? The fact that it seems to suggest schools do something that was not then happening indicates a desire to have it function as a target standard, but the list of things simply details out the parts of a larger expectation.

In that regard it seems more like a compliance standard that once met frees us to do a host of other things, or an imposed standard intended to define the minimum requirements, although again the lack of precision means it can't drive compliance and it can't serve to define the minimum requirements.

It doesn't specify performance, it doesn't explicitly shape anything, and it doesn't offer specificity in terms of definitions that will ensure it isn't mis-interpreted.

It does, however, sound great. After all, who could argue with the statement as a set of worthwhile things that schools should do?

They should, in fact, do all of these things and do them well, but elevating such an aphoristic statement to the level of a standard creates a whole host of questions: How would one meet such a standard? Is it a standard that every-one needs to meet in its entirety, or can strengths in one area make up for weaknesses in another? What would compliance look like for a school? How about a student? What proxies exist or would need to be created that would allow us to determine compliance? What does ethical understanding mean?

In spite of such difficult questions and obvious challenges regarding the implementation of such aphoristic standards, states chose the same pattern of standard creation as *A Nation at Risk* when they took on the role of building their own educational standards. In every instance, and in every case, states essentially broke large, aphoristic statements such as those in the *At Risk* standards into smaller and smaller chunks, and that process continues to the present.

The thinking seems to have been that the large, aphoristic standards lacked sufficient detail, and that detail would be the key to implementing a high-achieving system. But fulfillment standards—which these were clearly attempting to be—have to be *precise* in order to work. Simply taking yester-day's broad curriculum guides and elevating them to the level of a standard by breaking them into smaller and smaller pieces isn't likely to have the same effect.

It seems to me that another grammatical crime was committed here in that *detailed* and *precise* seem to have been somehow equated with one another, when—as was pointed out earlier—they reference very different characteristics of a thing, with *precision* representing a necessary level of exactness and *detailed* representing comprehensiveness.

Again, things can be precise and not detailed (target standards, for example), detailed but not precise (such as the educational standards being discussed), or detailed and precise (e.g., conformity standards).

The milieu of educational standards in which we currently operate are far more detailed than the *At Risk* standards, but just as imprecise. In Virginia, for example, high school standard 10.1 for reading is this:

> The student will participate in, collaborate in, and report on small-group learning activities.
>
> a. Assume responsibility for specific group tasks.
> b. Collaborate in the preparation or summary of the group activity.
> c. Include all group members in oral presentation.
> d. Choose vocabulary, language, and tone appropriate to the topic, audience, and purpose.
> e. Demonstrate the ability to work effectively with diverse teams to accomplish a common goal.
> f. Collaborate with others to exchange ideas, develop new understandings, make decisions, and solve problems.
> g. Access, critically evaluate, and use information accurately to solve problems.
> h. Evaluate one's own role in preparation and delivery of oral reports.
> i. Use a variety of strategies to listen actively.
> j. Analyze and interpret other's presentations.
> k. Evaluate effectiveness of group process in preparation and delivery of oral reports.

A statement that mirrors the *At Risk* statement precedes this list of statements (and the many more that follow):

> The tenth-grade student will become a skilled communicator in small-group learning activities. The student will examine, analyze, and produce media messages. The student will continue development of vocabulary, with attention to connotations, idioms, allusions, and evolution of language. The student will read and analyze literary texts from a variety of eras and cultures. Attention will be given to the analysis of nonfiction texts. The student will critique the writing of peers and professionals, using analysis to improve writing skills. The student will continue to build research skills by crediting sources and presenting information in a format appropriate for content. Grammar knowledge will be expanded as the student presents, writes, and edits materials, applying the conventions of language.[3]

This is just one example among thousands. Every state department of education website contains similar lists with the stated function of serving as educational standards in that state, and by and large they are both detailed and imprecise. Some have broad statements to which the label *standard* is actually applied, with smaller statements intended to articulate what the standard means, and others, like Virginia, name them all *standards*. All of them, however, follow a similar pattern to the Virginia version.

However compelling or rational the Virginia standards may be as statements we would like applied in the educational milieu, or however they are labeled or formulated, they are, first and foremost (and in spite of the level of detail), *imprecise*. I realize I'm harping on this point, but it really is critical. Lacking precision, state standards lack the adjudicating power that is the goal of fulfillment standards, make compliance difficult to envision, and given the difficulty in measuring them they require an outside proxy to set the criteria for success.

That is an odd sort of standard, indeed, one whose purpose remains, frankly, a bit elusive.

I for one would like to think that the creators of such standards *intended* them to be precise, intended for them to function as fulfillment standards, and that the imprecision is something of tragic accident. Here is why: standards that are *intentionally* imprecise serve as effective guides for a host of human interactions for activities that cannot be otherwise defined, but in the case of educational standards it appears that defining them was exactly the point. That is why it has to be something of an accident—*precision* had to have been the intent.

Imprecise standards are all around us. For example, my mother's constant reminder to her seven children to "be nice" was itself the declaration of a standard to which she fully expected us to comply, and despite the imprecision in it each of my brothers and sisters understood pretty well what she meant. The social makeup of the home and the look in my mother's eye made that so. The imprecision is what made it possible for my parents to establish a peaceful household based on a few principles rather than a thousand different rules.

My parents certainly could have made a ton of rules, but they wouldn't have been as effective; we were pretty smart kids and would have found a ton of loopholes and technicalities that we would have been all too happy to exploit. "Being nice" was much cleaner than a hundred exploitable rules that cannot possibly encompass the whole of seven children's potential naughtiness, and it served as a far more effective behavioral guide.

Lots of aspects of society work this way, including politeness, common courtesy, ethical behavior, and so on. Such imprecise standards—some that are written and others that exist only as common sense—help to establish the limits for all sort of behaviors as to what is or is not acceptable, and we should be grateful we have such a tool at our disposal. Imprecise *behavioral standards* are in fact much older than any industry or government standard, and it isn't hard to look around and find lots of examples of them in everyday life.

Unlike a fulfillment standard that contains within it the criteria for compliance (e.g., cars meeting the efficiency standard will average 50 miles per gallon by the year 2016; high schools will graduate 90 percent of incoming freshmen in four years), a behavioral standard requires that the judgment regarding compliance be positioned *outside* the standard. In the case of my mother's demand for niceness, the ability to render judgment was positioned—quite conveniently, I might add—in the hands of my parents.

This meant that as kids we were subject to a set of criteria that we often had to test in order to understand, since they were not very well defined. Or when they were a bit better defined, we might look for an opportunity to test the boundaries to see if we might get away with something and whatever the result add it to our understanding of the definition. The point is that as a tool for controlling a bunch of unruly kids, a behavioral standard was perfect. It could be a bit arbitrary and lack definition and still work beautifully.

In the case of societal standards for behavior, the definitions for what qualifies as compliance belong with society at large. I can attempt all I want to suggest that treating others with disdain or being intentionally rude meets societal expectations as I see them, but whether or not my behavior complies with standards for how we should treat each other is determined by how society at large interprets the standard.

Judgments of compliance may be from a single person or the whole of society, and even I may judge myself according to the criteria, but the criteria are not controlled or determined by me or even by the stated standard. The adjudicating criteria regarding compliance with a behavioral standard are always external to the standard itself.

Fulfillment and behavioral standards require very different approaches regarding the activities and behaviors that lead to compliance. Fulfillment standards are open to any and all possible ways in which the thing might be achieved, while behavioral standards explicitly constrain the choices one has. One engenders creative, out-of-the-box thinking, while the other explicitly limits it.

With fulfillment standards—even those designed to produce conformity or minimum acceptable thresholds—the goal is to comply as a means to opening up the possibility of being creative or of creating new opportunities. With behavioral standards the goal is to limit the universe of options to a manageable number. Thus a behavioral standard is always a bit about control—either by a parent or by society.

Consider as well how you expend energy in complying with the precision in a fulfillment standard and the imprecision in a behavioral standard. When a standard is precise it needs to be fulfilled so you expend energy to meet it and, once met, transfer most or all of that energy onto the next thing. The design of a fulfillment standard is such that it can be *exhausted*. It is entirely possible to look at a fulfillment standard and know when it is met, freeing you to move on to the next thing.

Complying with a behavioral standard requires a very different energy outlay: you must expend a fairly constant amount of energy every day in order to stay in compliance, since being nice yesterday and being nice today are two entirely different things. A behavioral standard is therefore *inexhaustible*: no matter how much energy you put toward the thing it can never be fully realized. That's what makes an imprecise behavioral standard such a powerful behavioral tool—it requires you to be constantly on your toes.

What happened in education was that a decision was made to bring to education all of the benefits that *fulfillment* standards have to offer, and yet the *behavioral* standard was selected as the means by which that was to be accomplished. What we are left with are hundreds of behavioral standards and an expectation that they can operate outside their design, as if they were not just detailed, but also precise.

Consider several mathematical standards, again from Virginia, but this time from grade eight, and within the content strand of Patterns, Functions, and Algebra:

> 8.14 The student will make connections between any two representations (tables, graphs, words, and rules) of a given relationship.
> 8.15 The student will
>
> > a) solve multistep linear equations in one variable with the variable on one and two sides of the equation;
> > b) solve two-step linear inequalities and graph the results on a number line; and
> > c) identify properties of operations used to solve an equation.
>
> 8.16 The student will graph a linear equation in two variables.
> 8.17 The student will identify the domain, range, independent variable, or dependent variable in a given situation. [4]

Each of these standards is certainly detailed, and just as certainly imprecise. None contain any criteria for adjudicating success, and thus they require that decision to come from elsewhere. Compliance with any of them are big, open-ended questions: How often? How much? To what degree? and more. Those answers aren't here.

As such, each of these statements has far more in common with a behavioral standard than a fulfillment standard—each is trying to get a student to *do* something as opposed to *achieve* something. Each is far more like a version of my parents telling me to be nice than a fulfillment standard regarding efficiency or effectiveness, the manufacture of a component part, or a minimum requirement.

As a guide to a curriculum they function just fine. As a standard requiring compliance they function quite poorly.

Each statement above certainly qualifies as a reasonable statement to guide the delivery of a school's curriculum, but when such statements are elevated to the role of a standard the statements are in fact asking for something very different: first, they ask for a school to set these and a hundred other statements up as the constraints for the educational enterprise, since a behavioral standard is designed to constrain to few acceptable choices.

Second, they ask a school to treat each as inexhaustible, creating a huge amount of cognitive dissonance in terms of what, when, and how to teach.

And third, because the standard is to be measured via an external proxy (in the case of reading and mathematics it is via a standardized test), it moves the adjudication of success outside the classroom, into a measure designed for another purpose, and beyond the people doing the hard work of actually teaching in what risks becoming a constrained and somewhat tiresome activity.

Indeed, what has in fact happened—whether intended or not—is that education has adopted hundreds of behavioral standards designed to constrain choices to a select few and demand constant attention, and then in turn asks that schools do great things well beyond those limitations and then again insists that the decisions regarding compliance be made elsewhere.

That inspires all sorts of odd behaviors. Curriculum directors over and over again must tie every aspect of the curriculum back to the standards with little to no ability to say when a standard has been met or complied with. In state after state (my home state of Texas being one of the worst offenders), weeks, even months of instructional time are lost to blatant test prep that offers zero pedagogical value for students but will hopefully assist in complying with the external metric.

Classes in arts and music have been scrapped so that the energy and resources can be put toward dozens of inexhaustible standards in reading and mathematics. Teachers are told that these standards must be a part of every class they teach—and educational publishers print hundreds of books each year that purport to show teachers how to do that.

Every state in this country now bases the quality determination for schools, classrooms, and more and more often, students, on standardized tests administered by each state, which always have been and always will be a distant proxy for achievement.

What the reform community believes it has done is a far cry from that. Their rhetoric treats the established standards as fulfillment standards, fully capable of launching educational achievement into the stratosphere while making it ever more efficient, while at the same time ensuring that the minimum requirements for a student to leave school are sufficient for that student to enter the worlds of college or work.

They insist that any failures are the fault of shortsighted, poorly trained, or just plain lazy teachers and administrators and have little to do with the system. They insist that if schools and teachers would just try harder and work smarter that the system will work.

This is absolutely the position taken by any number of policymakers and educational leaders, among them such educational superstars as Michele Rhee, formerly of Washington, D.C., and Joel Klein, formerly of New York City, to name just two of dozens. Each seems to presume that they had provided teachers and schools with a system of standards that were more than adequate—if only the teachers and administrators would just do their jobs—to justify putting in place systems to fire principals and teachers that they saw as underperforming.

The system, so they implied, is sufficiently robust to warrant the dismissal of those who cannot comply. That to me is an enormous amount of confidence to place in any system, and it assumes 100 percent confidence that the problem is elsewhere.

Federal policymakers seem to share that level of confidence in the system. As part of the hook for states to receive stimulus money during the recent recession to assist with their educational reforms (their words—not mine), the federal government insisted that the funds would be contingent upon a state's ability to tie student test scores that purport to be about these standards to teachers.

Even more recently, the Department of Education has encouraged that principal evaluations be based on the success of their teachers in such a system, and the trend toward additional impositions seems to be gaining steam.[5]

All of this is a huge amount of trust to place in a system that is so poorly understood. If some part of the system is off—and here we are not just talking about a part of the system but its foundation—then the system can never work as intended. If policymakers—as these gestures attempt—then hold people accountable for a set of results that the system was never designed to produce, you risk punishing others for your failure.

The educational reform community may not be conscious of the fact that educational standards in their current form don't function as intended, but the lack of precision in their use of the term *standard* suggests that deep down they sense it. *Standard* spends as much time as a rallying cry as it does referencing what it is.

Insisting that students, teachers, and schools must meet standards, must teach to standards, and in the end those standards are all that matter makes a person part of a reform-minded crew, and since standards are generally considered a good thing, who wouldn't want to be aligned with such thinking?

But consider the variety of meanings that encompasses:

- Standards as a broad, recognizable educational goal
- Standards as a test score on a standardized test (see next chapter)
- Standards as an imprecise, inexhaustible behavioral requirement
- Standard as something to be met, achieved, or fulfilled
- Standards-based education as a way of pointing to a form of education different from what went before
- Standards-based classrooms as a term that references someone who creates their instruction around the content statements

We can if we chose exist linguistically in a completely standards-based world and have no way of knowing precisely what that means.

I don't believe, however, that educational reformers have introduced a new type of standard or a new set of meanings for the word, comparable with what has happened in regard to *rigor*. *Standard* serves as a banner around which to rally the troops, but having rallied them offers only imprecision and confusion among its various meanings. *Rigor* might someday find one or more of its new meanings added to its present dictionary definitions, but no one seems to be attempting to redefine what a standard is or can do.

We seem to use *standard* in a manner that at least resembles its denotative meanings, but too often when we speak we seem to invoke one set of meanings while in fact referencing something else entirely.

We seem quite content to presume that we have invoked all the benefits in a fulfillment standard even though we established behavioral standards. And we know this because at the exact moment that the behavioral standards were established it was recognized that compliance would have to be determined via a proxy. Had they opted for fulfillment standards that would not have been the case.

What is remarkable is that very few people seem to be able to see just how poorly our system of education based on behavioral standards is working. Considering what actual fulfillment standards might have enabled is a sort of check on the system. This is, of course, a hypothetical argument, as such standards are not a part of education, but the differences are so stark that I think the point is relevant nonetheless.

Remember what the four types of fulfillment standards are supposed to enable:

1. Target standards open the door to a world of possibility for how to get a thing done. They are designed to foment creativity and innovation, and the quality of such a standard is judged by its ability to do just that. Industries that have established rich target standards have often been able to transform at a much more rapid pace than was previously thought possible.

2. Conformity standards standardize or define certain things in the name of efficiency to free resources to focus on more important things. Conformity standards allow for economies to grow at an accelerated pace by making the best use of limited resources, encouraging healthy competition in the marketplace, and helping maximize the value consumers receive. They are responsible for generating many of the efficiencies we enjoy in the marketplace today.

3. Imposed standards set limits or tolerances on things for the good of society. They serve as the floor for what is or is not acceptable, guaranteeing a minimum of quality for all of us.

4. A certification standard sets a person or an organization apart as having the capacity to get a thing done, thus creating trust of individuals or organizations that have earned the certification. As the numbers of certified individuals and organizations grow within an industry, trust for that industry has the opportunity to grow as well.

When I think of the educational landscape of the last twenty years during which behavioral educational standards have been the predominant tool for articulating what students should be able to do as a result of schooling, I don't notice a high level of creativity engendered by the movement, or efficiencies that allow us to more effectively use the ever more scarce resources available to run schools, or that we can declare the existence of a true educational floor designed to ensure that all students will be given an opportunity to succeed, or that the certification programs (i.e., "accountability" programs, in educational parlance) set up for teachers and schools have greatly increased our trust in the teaching profession.

What I think of instead is a "teach-to-the-test" mentality forced on teachers and administrators lest they lose their jobs, a reduction in arts and music education and those activities focused on our creative side, and curriculum writers who must justify every part of every lesson by showing how it supports one or more of the behavioral standards.

I think of the fact that according to the National Commission on Teaching and America's Future the teaching profession is losing almost half of its new teachers within the first five years,[6] and how we now trust teachers so little that many states are attempting to tie the annual increase in tested student achievement directly to a teacher[7] in spite of the fact that so many factors beyond schooling also have an impact on those scores.

And I think of the fact that when I first got involved with people in the educational standards movement this was the last thing any of us talked about as a reasonable future state. Our ideas were of something that was a far cry from this.

Had the educational reform community adopted fulfillment standards rather than behavioral standards—which would have frankly made sense because fulfillment standards align with what reformers were actually attempting to do—they would have had to accept the requirement that what was needed was standards that were *precise*.

Interestingly, precise fulfillment standards for education are not difficult to conjure with a little creativity, but they look profoundly different than what the educational community is accustomed to. Table 4.2 shows several examples of an educational fulfillment standard according to the categories of standards identified at the start of this chapter.

Table 4.2 shows several examples for each category of fulfillment standard. Each example is precise, contains within it the criteria for compliance, and can be measured and judged directly, without a proxy.

Note that the goal for each type of standard is *compliance*, with a benefit to follow: target standards are intended to impact the system or the student for the better the instant they are met.

Conformity standards standardize what needs to be in place in order to enable a great many other opportunities. Imposed standards set the threshold for expectations.

Certification standards are all something that schools or students choose to work toward and having met can show the world that they can be trusted to have accomplished something substantial. All of these are sufficiently precise as to be exhaustible: they can all be completed, and each can be measured directly, without a proxy.

These are, of course, just examples. But consider your own reaction to them. Regardless of whether your role is that of an educator, a parent, or just someone interested in the subject, the odds are you reacted in some fashion to each of these: you may have thought that some were silly, not high enough, ridiculously high, or just right. My point is that no matter your background or experience this type of standard means something similar to each of us.

You and I can debate the merits of each, you can add those you favor into the mix, and in the end the odds are that we could settle on a set of standards that could drive the exact types of activities we want in a school for our children and in which teachers could serve as the professionals they so desire to be. None of that is possible in our current standards environment.

Academics are, of course, a critical part of any of these standards—a rich academic environment is in fact the only way any of them can be accomplished. Imagine a school in which every student has to write well at least once each year—that is a higher *academic* standard than any with which I am

	Standards for Schools to Meet	Standards for Students to Meet
Target Standards—standards that schools and students can and should work towards and if they do fundamentally improve the quality of the school or the quality of the education being earned	• 80% of students graduate within four years of entering high school, and 90% within five • 90% of teachers in the building longer that five years will have an advanced degree or a National Teacher Certification	• Successful participation in three or more Advanced Placement or International Baccalaureate courses • Accurate completion of 80% of the stretch goals included with weekly mathematics assignments • Successful participation in planning and carrying out three out of the five annual academic service projects
Conformity Standards—the enabling standards that set the stage for additional learning and growth	• 90% of classes are taught by staff trained in the subject matter and the developmental level of their students • Teachers and faculty will participate in accredited content-based training or education of the educator's choice for a minimum of three days annually • Learning materials are current, up to date, and represent approaches sanctioned by leading researchers and scholars	• All students will read at a fluency rate of x words per minute by x grade • All students will produce a well wrought piece of writing once each year without time as the constraint • All students will complete a complex analysis involving mathematical concepts in each year of schooling, without time as the constraint
Imposed Standards—the baseline thresholds and expectations	• Annually, each teacher will create and deliver to their peers two 1/2 hour training sessions focused directly on student work are working towards to be delivered during department meetings • School leaders will create an environment that gives each teaches the capacity to deliver individualized instruction to students that need it or want it for a minimum of six hours each week	• In order to graduate, do one of the following: 1. Conduct a short play and put it on outside regular school hours 2. Put on an art exhibition displaying no fewer than six original pieces created by the student 3. Perform for an audience of not fewer than 20—alone or with 1-3 other students—three or more works of music by a known artist or composer
		• Each student that matriculates from one grade cluster to the next will have taught a mathematical concept to a small group of younger students, assigned and corrected their homework, and worked with the students to correct misunderstandings
Certification standards—the indicators of achievement (these are chosen—no sanctions apply for non-compliance)	• Schools can work towards a variety of accreditation programs; arts magnet, science magnet, high academics, etc.	• Students that double the number of graduation standards met will earn an honorary diploma • Advanced Placement Diploma • International Baccalaureate Diploma

Table 4.2. Educational Fulfillment Standards

familiar, and it cannot be accomplished absent a rich *academic* environment in which teachers can guide students in the process of achieving it.

Just as importantly, none of the hypothetical standards in the chart is textbook or curriculum dependent, so unlike content statements such as those contained in state standards that take years to make it into classrooms, fulfillment standards can be set today and start having an immediate impact.

That is one of the real beauties of fulfillment standards: establish one today and it generates positive, meaningful activity tomorrow. This is perhaps the single best way to know that the standards route we've chosen cannot meet the promise of education—if it takes half of a student's academic career to make a change, and that change is deemed to be critical to the student's and the country's success, we have failed at the very least a generation of students and haven't done the nation any favors either.

Higher standards echo as one of the clarion calls in the reform world (often in the suggestion that we need "more rigorous" standards, which I find wonderfully ironic—the statement is intended to mean something along the lines of tougher, more strident, or some such stuff, while I want them to be more precise, which actually is a part of the actual definition—thus, on this point, we "agree").

States compare and attempt to show how their standards are just as high if not higher than their neighbors or those that guide the National Assessment of Educational Progress (NAEP). Part of the justification for states to adopt the new Common Core standards is the claim that they are higher (again, the claim that they are "more rigorous") than what went before. What is being compared, of course, are sets of behavioral aphoristic standards, which is a nearly impossible intellectual challenge when you think about it.

Context has to be a part of understanding the differences between behavioral standards. Remember that even when the same terms are used that the context and therefore the interpretation can differ dramatically. My parents saying "be nice" and your parents saying "be nice" may or may not be referring to the same thing. My parents, for example, had seven children, so "be nice" often meant don't hit and don't break things. For my friends that were only children it meant those things plus an admonition to be polite and not run around the house like those crazy Tanner kids.

Answering the question as to who had the higher standard depends: if all you are interested in are the number of things in the interpretation, then the parents of the only child win because their definition included more things, but if what matters is the end results in terms of actual behavior, my parents could make a case that controlling seven kids is a far greater challenge than controlling one.

Behavioral standards in education are just as hard to compare. We can compare at the semantic level and count the number of requirements or compare the number of active verbs or determine which set of standards introduces the greatest number of concepts. We can perform a more formal analysis (lots of organizations actually do this) that rates each statement for each of several criteria such that those ratings can be summarized and reported, but the imprecision in such analyses is rather startling, and thus no matter the methodology, such analyses tend to be of limited value.

They tend to ignore the fact that what are being described in the statements are lots of student behaviors and that the meaning behind those behaviors will depend on the context in which they receive an interpretation. That is the case with any aphoristic statement. We could have a grade four standard that seems as straightforward as "students will comprehend what they read," but it must then be interpreted through the context of the school, and the context can vary by a great deal, just as the contexts for "be nice" do.

Consider a school in an upper-middle-class neighborhood with big houses and nice lawns, and imagine the elementary school building you would expect to see in the middle of it. Now imagine a poor, suburban neighborhood with an unacceptably high crime rate, a high incidence of homelessness, and the elementary school in the middle of it, where 99 percent of the students qualify for the federal breakfast and lunch subsidy.

The simple fact is that while teachers in both schools may have the same job description, the behavioral comprehension standard will be interpreted within two very different contexts—even when the two teachers have the exact same expectation regarding it. The teacher in a wealthier school is more likely to have a smaller class size, to have more individual time with each student, and to be able to count on more support at home to help with homework, than the teacher in a disadvantaged school.

The teacher in the latter school is more likely to have a higher rate of absenteeism, a lower rate of homework completion, and will have to devote at least some time every day dealing with the social and emotional needs of students that probably don't exist to the same degree in the wealthier school.

In a reform environment the idea was to ensure that all of the students in both these classrooms had a shot at the same standards, but if that was the case then behavioral standards were the wrong model because such a model actually requires a context for interpretation, meaning that the context cannot help but interfere.

In the poor school the number of issues that must be addressed to ensure that a child is even ready or able to learn are simply greater than in the rich school. The wealthy school, because of the luck of the draw, has more time and energy to devote to the issue, making it so much easier to add a richer interpretation to the standard, while the poor school, without an influx of additional teaching resources, does not.

In the end, attempting to determine who truly had the higher standard is impossible. It may be the teacher in the wealthier school who had far fewer challenges to address, or it may be the teacher in the disadvantaged school where none of the children quite made it but the progress, by any measure, may have been stunning.

(Of course, in the real world we would administer a standardized test to answer the question, which is even more decontextualized than a behavioral standard and equally problematic—for now, however, I'll stick to the standards.)

In both schools, what would it mean to raise the standards, and how would you go about it? That is a hard one for me. If, as the common interpretation now goes, it means that the poor school just needs to try harder, that troubles me. My hypothetical teacher (and so many amazing real teachers in just that situation) are all working as hard as they can to do the best they can in next to impossible situations and doing, in so many instances, an admirable job.

What bothers me even more is that we have a system of behavioral standards that were created under the implied assumption that the behaviors as described would be interpreted under similar conditions, which allow policymakers to infer that they mean the same thing to everyone. It is as if I could repeat the old aphorism "less is more" absent a context and expect it to mean the same thing to all of us.

That sort of ethnocentric behavior by policymakers allows them to give lip service to the notion of *all students* without the hard thinking as to what a standard for *all students* actually looks like. Behavioral standards can only be applied the same *for all kids* when *all kids* face the some socioeconomic conditions when they wake up in the morning, and the last I checked we aren't yet at that point.

If the goal of reform was to create standards that mattered the same for all students, those standards needed to be such that the context didn't matter. I truly believe that was the goal for the standards movement, but we missed it.

Fulfillment standards don't suffer from these problems or the prerequisite that in order to work we must first solve a problem that has plagued society for as long as we've been a society. Fulfillment standards can be interpreted the same regardless of context, and the achievement of a fulfillment standard indicates what thing was accomplished irrespective of location.

Consider the simplest (and one of my favorite) examples of a fulfillment standard for students: a student will write an exemplary paper before the end of each year of school. I know that such a standard can be applied equally in any of my hypothetical schools, with the only difference being in the number of students that achieve it, and yet still the standard is the same. If doubts arise that the expectations aren't aligned, I can ask for the work from both schools and compare it with my own eyes. When the schools differ in the number of children who achieve it, I can attribute the difference to the context, but the expectation is the same, and if I want a different outcome I cannot simply tell teachers in the poorer school to try harder.

Fulfillment standards—unlike behavioral statements—can be raised the instant the old standard is deemed insufficient. If it was sufficient yesterday to graduate 80 percent of your students within four years, and now we need that number to be 90 percent, we have a higher standard. If we add a requirement to the teacher certification process, that process is now more challenging to meet. If we ask students to achieve the stretch goals on their homework more frequently than before in order to qualify for an honorary distinction, achieving that standard now means more than it did before.

None of these or any fulfillment standard requires the context to be fixed before they can be achieved or raised. A poor school is just as capable of working toward them as a rich school, and when a standard is raised it means the same thing to everyone.

The next chapter regarding educational standards has already begun, fraught with all the perils of the last one. The leaders of state educational systems and governors came to the conclusion several years back that among the things that ailed education was the fact that states were each working with different mathematics and reading content standards, not the fact that the system of educational standards might be fundamentally flawed.

The result is the recently developed Common Core standards released by the National Governor's Association and the Council of Chief State School Officers. [8]

These standards are now the basis for massive investment by publishers preparing textbooks and materials to sell to schools and a $330 million investment by the federal government to build standardized tests based on that content. A great many states have agreed to adopt the Common Core standards as their own, and while the jury is still out as to whether or not they will eventually serve as the backbone for American education envisioned by those who championed them and still do, they are at the very least a major force at present.

The statements that make up the standards are a bit of a full circle back to those in *A Nation at Risk*. Consider a randomly picked reading standard:

> CCSS.ELA-Literacy.RL.9-10.2 Determine a theme or central idea of a text and analyze in detail its development over the course of the text, including how it emerges and is shaped and refined by specific details; provide an objective summary of the text. [9]

The flavor is exactly that of the *At Risk* standard: a detailed behavioral statement that lacks any degree of precision, and all of the Common Core follows a similar pattern. These standards, like their predecessors, will again require a context in which it can be interpreted, meaning that the interpretations will differ according to the different contexts, and they again require an external proxy judgment regarding compliance.

The assumption seems to be that what is wrong with the state standards that have been used for the past ten to fifteen years was the *substance*, but the *form* itself was just fine. At no point is there any evidence that the form the standards should take was a part of the discussion.

The threshold for the Common Core standards to transform education is every bit as high as what now exists for state standards, as they, too, will require that our societal ills can somehow be made not to matter in order for that to happen.

Like their predecessors, these new behavioral statements may offer a much improved and much needed set of guidelines for a rich curriculum, but that doesn't mean they are also qualified to serve as standards that can transform the educational enterprise. They lack the level of specificity by which successful standards have in fact caused such transformations, and wishing and hoping that standards that follow the exact same formula as their predecessors can do what their predecessors could not is to fail to learn from history.

Our at-risk students will continue to be at the mercy of the socioeconomic climes where they go to school, and education reformers will again have two choices when educational achievement falls short of expectations: blame the system they created or blame teachers.

NOTES

1. Interestingly, this could be the reason the term *rigor* was introduced to the educational enterprise, since meeting a standard can only be determined by a measure that is rigorously applied. Standards for what qualifies as an energy-efficient light bulb or for safe working conditions in a coalmine or the size of a battery must be rigorously applied in order to determine compliance. That means that as an adjective describing how standards should be applied, the term *rigor* functions just fine. But to say that a standard is good because it is rigorous offers a way to join a community of those who believe standards should be rigorous without a sense of what that really means.

2. The example here comes from a journal entry I wrote following a dinner some twenty years ago at which a similar story was told. Phil Daro and Sally Hampton, two early mentors, had the discussion while I just sat and listened. If memory serves, Phil gets the credit for telling the story. Any missteps in what he told versus my hypothetical version included here are my own.

3. *Standards of Learning*, Virginia Department of Education. http://www.doe.virginia.gov/testing/sol/standards_docs/english/2010/stds_english10.pdf, accessed April 8, 2013.

4. *Standards of Learning*.

5. Wayne Riddle and Nancy Kober, *What Impact Will NCLB Waivers Have on the Consistency, Complexity and Transparency of State Accountability Systems?* (Washington, DC: Center for Education Policy, 2012), 1.

6. National Commission on Teaching and America's Future, "Nation's Schools Facing Largest Teacher Retirement Wave in History," June 24, 2001. http://nctaf.org/announcements/nations-schools-facing-largest-teacher-retirement-wave-in-history/, accessed April 8, 2013.

7. Riddle and Kober, *What Impact Will NCLB Waivers Have*, 1.

8. These two groups were at the forefront in the effort to create common standards in reading and mathematics. They continue to lead and drive most of that effort.

9. Common Core State Standards Initiative, "English Language Arts Standards Grades 9–10." http://www.corestandards.org/ELA-Literacy/RL/9-10/2, accessed April 8, 2013.

Chapter Five

Standardized Tests

A colleague of mine in the testing field (in which I have spent the bulk of my career) once said to me that testing is the way we measure the quality of education in this country and that people who didn't like that needed to get over it. From a pragmatic perspective you would have to admit that he was right.

In the reform paradigm in particular, standardized test results represent the means by which we adjudicate student and school performance against the existing content standards. Test data are not just the most cited of any educational performance data, they are the most misunderstood, and by far, the most misused.

In fact, tests have come to play just about any role a policymaker wishes to assign to them without so much as even a rudimentary understanding of what a standardized test is, what it was designed to do, or how it was designed to be used. A standardized test score now determines whether a student has sufficiently learned his or her assignments, whether a teacher has effectively delivered the curriculum, whether a principal is or is not a fit instructional leader, and whether the system of education is functioning as intended.

None of these was ever inferred in the design. Choosing such an instrument and deploying it counter to its design has serious consequences.

Before I begin an exploration of what a standardized test is and how they work, let me first say this: when I offer criticisms in regard to such tests, it is of the manner in which such tests are used. In the hands of a thoughtful practitioner or a researcher, a well-designed, properly administered standardized test can produce results that serve alongside a variety of measures for helping to understand the complexities of schooling and what might be done to advance the education of a school's assigned students.

In the hands of an ill-informed individual, the scores from that same test serve as a blunt instrument that can thwart the best designed educational plans, stunt a student's ability to grow, and offer a judgment of a teacher or school administrator that stands a high probability of being dead wrong. It is these problems that I hope to address.

A well-built standardized test is actually pretty remarkable in terms of its design and function. Let's start with those that I took when I was a kid—not as a point of nostalgia, but as the starting point to a story.

As I approach my fifties, those in my generation certainly remember the standardized tests that were an annual part of schooling. It was a ritual during which we would be handed a test booklet, an answer document, and a #2 pencil. Some months later we would be handed a piece of paper that suggested how our performance ranked among students throughout the country. When it got lost in our backpacks, our parents rarely noticed that anything was missing.

Those test scores were proxies for what had happened throughout the school year. They didn't come close to measuring the whole of what happened, but rather, they offered a specific sample of the content designed to allow for an inference from the limited content to a much larger domain. It was an inexpensive way to gather some empirical data regarding our performance as students, classrooms, and schools.

The questions that were selected for inclusion were incredibly important in terms of a variety of properties, most notably for their ability to *discriminate* among a variety of student performances, not because the material somehow had anything to do with the curriculum.

The point of such tests was to show the differences within a population of students. That would allow you to see how students stacked up against their peers at the school, district, state, and national levels. The results were sophisticated enough that educators were able to see how certain segments of their students were performing compared to other similar schools so that what worked in one place could, at least in theory, be transferred to another.

In order for the comparisons to work, it was imperative that the tests be given under conditions that are sufficiently similar so that the results of test takers or groups of test takers can be compared.

As an example, it wouldn't be very fair to compare my test score to yours if my teacher forgot to erase yesterday's lesson from the board but yours did, since I may be able to benefit in a way you cannot. Our results couldn't be compared because they would mean different things: yours would indicate what you knew, but mine may or may not do the same depending on whether or not I gleaned an answer from the board.

To say that one of us did better or worse would be inappropriate—the fact is we could not say with any degree of surety if that is or is not the case.

While standardization ensured that our test scores could be compared, it was the selection of the test items that actually enabled those comparisons. This is actually a fairly easy process to imagine (though I apologize to those in the measurement community for making it sound this simple, as in practice it most certainly is not, and there is a great more to it).

Consider that the perfect item to help me divide a room full of people into two groups—those who answered the item correctly and those who did not—is one that also divided a similar room full of people into two groups. I could then administer that item to the new roomful of people and have a reasonable expectation that the performance in the new room would at least be similar to the performance in the original room.

If the room I want to test consists of thirty people, however, I have limited information regarding the two sets of people identified by my one-item test. I can get more information about the makeup of the group if I add a second item with similar properties to my test, as now I have a chance at three groups of people emerging: those who miss both items, those who answer one right and one wrong, and those who answer both correctly. A third item gives me four groups, and so on and so on.

By the time I get to somewhere between thirty to forty items, I have my test. I could, if I wanted to, continue to add items, but at some point I wind up with more groups than are useful. That's why most standardized tests were in the thirty-to-forty-item range—that's an optimal number that gives the maximum amount of information for the smallest amount of effort.

That number of items would allow me to divide the room into enough groups so that I could rank the test takers from the highest performing to the lowest performing based on the number of items each person answered correctly, giving me a view of the room's performance.

With my hypothetical test, I can now go to lots of other rooms full of people in order to see how they compare to each other. Some rooms will do much better than others, and some will do worse.

And interestingly enough, certain patterns will emerge that can only be seen if I look at the number of people in a group scoring at each possible score total. For example, I could have two rooms that both averaged getting half the items correct, but one was because everyone earned the same score that was also the average, while in the other because half the room answered them all correctly and half answered them all incorrectly.

Clearly those two rooms are profoundly different, and my hypothetical standardized test is just the sort of tool to help me see that.

Standardized tests such as the Stanford Achievement Test, the Iowa Test of Basic Skills, or the California Achievement Test—which were commercially available tests when I was in school—were also *norm-referenced* tests, which had to do with an additional point of comparison they provided.

Prior to publication, but after the selection of test items that met the criteria described above, test publishers would administer their tests as a study to a nationally representative sample of students, and from that work add a level of reporting that would show how each student compared to the national sample.

That way, if I was told that I was at the seventy-fifth percentile in science, that meant that on the test I took that my performance was better than 75 percent of the students that participated in that national study. In this way I had a basis for comparison that made sense with only minimal explanation.

Note, however, what was not on the tests of my youth: items that everyone would answer correctly, or items that everyone would answer incorrectly. The reason for this was simple: they didn't contribute to understanding the distribution of people across all of the possible scores.

If every single test taker answered an item correctly, it contributed nothing to an understanding of the differences within the group. So, too, with an item that everyone would answer incorrectly. And since the point of these standardized tests was to quickly and efficiently understand how the people in a room and across the various rooms compare, adding items that didn't assist with that was a waste of both time and resources.

As such, the standardized tests I took as a kid were curriculum *independent*, meaning that they could do what they were designed to do regardless of the curriculum being taught. In fact, it would have been utter foolishness to limit the curriculum to a set of test items that were selected with the criteria that roughly half the students that answered them would do so incorrectly.

That meant that some of the most basic, fundamental content wouldn't be included, since nearly everyone would answer those items correctly, and the most challenging content would be excluded, since very few were likely to answer those items correctly.

It should be clear that the criteria for what has to be included in a standardized test and what should be included in a rich curriculum are very different, with one having to do with selecting the content most likely to show a distribution of students as of a date certain, and the other having to do with being the best selection to facilitate learning throughout the school year.

The content in the items on a test, in fact, didn't matter nearly as much as most people would imagine. They were selected because they made for a reasonable *proxy* for something much more difficult to measure, not because they represented the most critical components within a domain. To alter instruction according to what was or was not included on a standardized test would have been absurd.

The function of the test was such that content at the two ends of the spectrum is superfluous to its purpose, and even the items that made it weren't designed to influence or guide the curriculum. The function of teaching was (and is) to explicitly go after the full range of material provided in the curriculum. The classroom was intended to function independent from the testing experience, and the test was intended to function independent of what happened in classrooms.

In fact, the test was designed to work *only if* it could function independent of the classroom. The best way for me to explain why involves using the eye exam at the Department of Motor Vehicles to illustrate: allowing the content of a standardized test to ever become the basis for teaching would be akin to studying for the eye exam you take when applying for a driver's license. You may be able to pass the test, but it won't mean anything.[1]

I actually have some personal experience with this through my grandmother, who admitted to my mother in her later years that she couldn't pass the eye test and so just listened to others answer the questions and repeated what they said. It worked—my grandmother kept her license.

My mother learned that her mother really couldn't see very well when she realized that rather than looking for the light to change she looked at the drivers in front of her or to her side as the signal for when it was time to go. My grandmother passed her driver's test, but because she "studied" for it, it didn't mean a thing.

While it may seem extreme to argue that studying for a standardized test and studying for an eye test would be two versions of the same thing, I assure you it is not. An eye test is only useful when it can reference something beyond itself: eyesight.

The clerk behind the counter at the DMV cannot be counted on to have sufficient medical training to conduct a medical exam to determine the quality of an applicant's eyesight. They need a reasonable proxy that can be quickly administered to an applicant. Having an applicant read the letters on a wall is a reasonable proxy, but only if the applicant uses sight and not their hearing or their wits (my grandmother obviously lacked for neither of these).

A standardized test was only useful when it referenced something beyond itself through its rankings: student achievement. School administrators or researchers would find it a real challenge to provide a reasonable summary of the impact of the educational process for every student in a school. They found in standardized, norm-referenced tests a reasonable proxy for what they were not themselves capable of providing otherwise.

Rank ordering students and comparing their performance relative to the rest of the country provided a reasonable proxy, but only if students took the test under standardized conditions, meaning that the instruction was not altered in anticipation of it, and the tests were administered in a similar fashion.

If the eye test is only about itself, which is what my grandmother made it when she "studied" for it, she proved she could pass it without seeing. If a standardized test is only about itself, it becomes possible to do well on it by just studying a similar set of test items. Scores from either, under those conditions, would be meaningless in regard to the target of the measure.

Any attempt to anticipate the content in a standardized test destroyed the ability to provide a comparison, which is the purpose for administering such a thing in the first place. If a teacher or a school taught to the test and then attempted to find any sort of meaning in those scores, they were being delusional.

If you were in a classroom where the test had explicitly been made the curriculum, and I were in a classroom where the curriculum was comprised of rich learning experiences that we all agreed represents a meaningful and challenging curriculum, our test results could not be compared because they would not have meant the same thing.

Your test score answered the question regarding how effectively you prepped for the test. My test score would have answered the question regarding how I ranked against others.

To compare the scores would have risked the assumption that you outperformed me when in fact I was exposed to a far richer curriculum and performed at a far higher level than you, but your test score was higher since you, in effect, were given the answers.

Or if I outperformed you, the risk is that your score would not be seen as evidence that your classroom should toss out the test-based curriculum and adopt one that is full and rich like what I was exposed to, but rather, since you missed items that appear to be fairly easy, the solution may appear to be to drill you even harder on that simple content, further reifying the bad system in which you were trying to receive an education.

Teaching to the test is delusional because the test items were selected specifically because roughly half of the students would answer them correctly and half would answer them incorrectly, meaning that the drill approach on tested content is always destined to fall a bit short.

No matter how much the curriculum might have focused on the tested content, the odds were that some of the items would still be missed—that was a part of the criteria for why they were chosen in the first place.

The danger of drilling was that drilling begets more drilling, since the content appeared so simple that common sense seemed to suggest that students were missing items because they lacked the knowledge located in specific items. Again, the items were selected so that as a group they could present a test that could be compared to others. To focus on a single item would have been to deny the reason it was selected for inclusion, which had nothing to do with suggesting anything regarding instruction.

That is why teaching to the test is akin to studying for the eye exam at the DMV: no good can ever come of it. This is not to say that it didn't happen. My grandmother was no doubt not the only sight-impaired person to figure out how to pass an eye test without being able to see, and as norm-referenced tests started to really take hold in schools the opportunities for misuse increased dramatically, and unfortunately teaching to the test and other forms of gaming the system emerged as a real concern.

One can argue the merits of whether or not the standardized test instruments of my youth served as a helpful educational tool—I won't bother with that argument here (though at one point in my career I worked on the Stanford Achievement Test, Tenth Edition, so where I would fall in the argument probably wouldn't surprise you). What I will offer is that the point was always that the limit of such tests was that they could serve as a proxy for a much larger set of activities that were, by definition, not a part of the test.

As a proxy, they could offer their comparisons in a fair and reasonable manner, but they could only do that under the explicit agreement with teachers and schools that they function independent of the curriculum.

Fast-forward thirty (or so) years to the present, and a great deal has changed: the content for our tests no longer comes from publishers but from state standards documents, many states use a variety of question types in addition to multiple-choice items, and the test scores are no longer reported as a percentile (e.g., "your child is in the seventy-sixth percentile") but as a category with names such as *proficient*, *meets the standard*, and others.

In addition, a huge change has occurred regarding how test scores are used: they are, quite literally, the single most prominent (and often the only) indicator of educational quality for students, teachers, and principals, with serious consequences for poor performance. Now everybody cares about the results, including policymakers, real estate agents, mayors, newspaper publishers, and governors, to name just a few.

Education reformers have tried on some new labels for this new generation of tests, such as *criterion-referenced*, or even *standards-based*, indicating the source for the content.

One of the greatest changes is that the tests are now used to inform curriculum and instruction, counter to what their predecessors did. In fact, the No Child Left Behind regulations explicitly require that test scores from a spring test be returned prior to the start of the school year in the fall so that they can be used to inform instruction.[2]

Our policy now enshrines the idea that the tests are no longer curriculum independent because the content comes from state standards as opposed to test publishers.

What education reformers and policymakers failed to do, however, was select an underlying assessment design that matched their intent. They may have wanted a design that was curriculum *dependent* to better align teaching and testing, and they may have wanted one that had to do with allowing for a redefinition of what educational achievement really means, but if that was the case then they should have selected a design that matched that intent.

They did not. Instead, they opted for the basic design of the tests from my childhood, put in a few minor tweaks, and then offered it to an unsuspecting public as something that was very much new and improved.

The evidence that not much has changed is frankly overwhelming, most notably: the test items are still selected for their ability to discriminate performance within a population, and the goal is still to administer them under standardized conditions so that the results can be compared within and among populations of students, not because the content is the most important or the most relevant from an instructional perspective.

You don't need to take my word for this, but look instead at the technical reports most states produce each year that offer the details regarding their assessments and how they were constructed. [3]

It is simply a basic tenet of educational measurement that an item that fails in its ability to help discriminate in terms of performance is a useless item for the purposes of this "new" brand of test. The failure to select a different design for measuring achievement means that all of the same restrictions should still apply in order for the results to mean anything: most notably that tests should operate in the background, and the tested content must not be anticipated or taught to in any way.

The tests, separated by thirty years and little else, now operate as if they have been magically transformed, as if some political sorcerer had the power to wave a wand and make it so.

What is designed to be a curriculum-independent test instrument with its interpretive power limited to providing a sense of where schools and students rank relative to their peers now operates well outside and beyond that design and serves as the primary source for curricular change and the ultimate indicator regarding the quality of schools.

That is an act of sorcery stunning for its bravado, its arrogance, and its ignorance.

There seems to me, however, to be an even larger and more pervasive issue regarding the design of these tests when considering the futures of the children education serves, and our country at large: the tests are only designed to provide a sense of how things are, not how things can or should be.

When I look at a group's test scores, I am looking at a statistical approximation of how things are, of the status quo for that population. Remember that the test is assembled of items selected for their ability to discriminate student performances. The items that make it into the test, then, are those that an "average" student is just as likely to answer right as wrong. Every statistic that goes into the creation of the test is based upon the current status of things, not upon some future, better state. At no point do you ask, "What do we want things to be like in the future?" That is not a part of the design.

That means that when I look at the items that allowed for the approximation to be made, I am looking at items that enabled me to see what the status quo looks like—one that places a set of artificial limits on the tested material so that it is capable of providing those estimates. Thus a question: If the tests and their results offer a snapshot of the status quo, what would be the consequences of using that definition as the basis for an education? The answer: You aren't going to see much in the way of change.

It would be counterintuitive to think that if you teach to any representation of the "way things are" you have a shot at getting to someplace different, someplace better, since "different" and "better" are external to any current representation of the status quo, and they are not on the test—by design.

That may sound like philosophical mumbo jumbo, but it is not. Teaching to the status quo will get you more of the same. That is just plain common sense.

At least in the good old days we were transparent about what the tests represented. (I'm not trying to be nostalgic here—just factual.) We added norms to exams, meaning that we went out of our way statistically to ensure that the set of test scores to which students were being compared indeed represented the status quo of the nation.

That way a student, classroom, or school could see where they fit relative to where everyone else was at the moment. But the goal for moving forward was to improve against the status quo, to rise in comparison to it, which meant doing the things educationally that were outside and beyond the status quo, and certainly the test. To entrench a school or a student in simply replicating the status quo would have been a good way to halt any sort of improvement.

The reality of what is at the heart of our tests is now masked by how we report the scores. Rather than report scores as a percentile rank, we now report a range of scores with words—*proficient, meets the standard, below the standard*—but for all practical purposes the latter is just a less precise version of the former.

The words may trick us into thinking that some level of aspiration is identified by the test, but that doesn't change what the test is: it is an instrument designed to approximate the status quo of a population so that a person or school's position relative to the status quo can be identified.

"Meeting" a standard in such a test could be said to be a proxy for what happened outside or beyond the test, but that is a huge reach. First, odds are that the test scores were manipulated by serving as the basis for at least some instruction, and second, even if they weren't that sort of inference would always need to be treated as the imprecise estimate it couldn't help but be.

We should give great pause to whether or not our inability to see significant advances in student achievement is because of our obsession with standardized test scores. The idea of reform was all about the idea of moving well

beyond the status quo, of launching student achievement into the stratosphere, and doing so for all students.

And then an instrument is selected that is all about the status quo and
one's position within it. Material that operates outside the status quo—which
represents the very goal of the reform movement—is not a part of the instru-
mentation.

Worse, the seemingly simple nature of the test items that make it to the
test—that about half of the "average" students will miss—have become the
basis for teaching because of the misperception that those items are "easy"
and students need to learn that material before moving on to more challenging content.

Each year those items are replaced by other seemingly simple items—
again selected because half of the average students will miss them—and
when the average students again miss those in fairly large numbers that
seems to suggest that once again educators have failed to teach even the most
basic of content.

If we fail to provide access for all students to the most meaningful educational material, we will have missed a primary goal of reform. If we limit our
thinking to test content that has never—by design—been worthy of or intended to have anything to do with instruction—we risk the reduction of the
curriculum to the content of a standardized test, which is the path many now
mistakenly believe the reform instrument has indicated is appropriate.

Nothing could be further from the truth, or more outside the design that
underlies such instruments, but the more we think it so the more likely we are
to repeat an unsatisfactory present while attempting to do otherwise.

Part of the reason for having forgotten what a test is and how it works—or
perhaps we never really knew—is certainly due to the seductive nature of a
number. We are a nation that attributes all sorts of meaning and trust to
numbers—from the state of the financial markets to the gross domestic product to the price of milk or a gallon of gas—without a clue as to how such
numbers are actually computed.

We trust in such numbers to such an extent that we interpret rises and falls
in such things to be harbingers of doom or a signal of goodness and strength,
adding a sense of value to the change: when the stock market rises it's a good
thing, but when the price of a gallon of milk goes up that is bad.

We feel comfortable doing this because while most of us have no clue
how such numbers are produced, deep inside we doubt that anyone would
have a reason to manipulate them—even if they had the power to do so—
since doing so would produce a false sense of the state of things, which risks
a whole series of bad or inappropriate decisions as a result.

Test scores are a natural extension of that thinking. They allow us to
reduce the entire educational enterprise into a few numbers that can then

offer judgment on a school. When the scores go up, we act pleased, as if rising test scores are always an indicator of good things, and when they go down, we are disappointed, since a decline in scores indicates that the school has failed to live up to its promise.

What each of these numbers—including test scores and the GDP—has in common is absolute silence as to the cause of any change, and thus absolute silence as to whether or not the change represents something good or bad.

The changes in them from one set of results to the next are no different than your blood pressure reading from your last physical. You may have high or low blood pressure, or your blood pressure may be trending higher or lower, but nowhere in the blood pressure reading is a reason for the change or the condition to be found.

That determination is exterior to the measure. You may be overweight, or extremely stressed, or be under care of a physician and on blood pressure medicine that finally kicked in to get things under control. GDP can rise or fall for hundreds of reasons, and the price of a gallon of milk is the result of a huge combination of factors that can only be examined outside the final indicator of its value.

Test scores are unique in this regard, because for some strange reason we overtrust them to such an extent that we treat them as self-evident, as if the cause either doesn't matter or is so simple that it becomes an "any idiot ought to be able to see" type of problem.

Overtrusting a test score allows us to interpret a rising test score as always good and a falling test score as always bad without regard to an interpretive lens, when educating a student is just as complex an activity as interpreting the causes behind a change in GDP.

In the days of my childhood, a test score could suggest that I was in the seventy-fifth percentile in a particular subject area, meaning that when compared to a nationally representative sample of students I performed better than three-fourths of those students and worse than about a quarter, but it cannot offer any opinions regarding the complexities for how I got there.

Was I a high-performing student that just didn't care? A struggling student who really gave it my all during the past year? Was I in a classroom that drilled me on the tested content so that the score indicates little more than the effectiveness of an impoverished educational strategy, or was I exposed to a rich curriculum that ignored the fact that a test would be given at the end of the year, allowing the score to serve as the proxy it was designed to provide?

And if my ranking changed from one year to the next, to what was that due? A better or worse curriculum? A test-based curriculum that limited teaching to the tested content? A teacher that I liked or disliked more than the last one? Maturity? The fact that I had a great year regarding learning, or a lousy one? Was it the fault of my teacher? My parents? Or a personal tragedy or triumph that inspired me or hindered me throughout the year?

Any standardized test score, and any change in a test score over time, is absolutely silent as to its cause. The assumption that a rising test score is always caused by good things is just plain false, just as is the assumption that a falling test score is always indicative of the failure of a school.

Scores can rise, fall, or stay the same for a variety of reasons, which is why they require a context in which to be interpreted. A test score can be made to rise from one year to the next as a result of practices that are educationally sound, like ignoring the fact that the test exists and teaching a rich curriculum, or it can be made to rise by limiting the curriculum to the test, thereby damaging a student's long-term chances for educational success.

A school can hold steady in terms of test scores through a rapid shift in its demographic to a poorer and more diverse population to which it is accustomed and through a rich curriculum serve its students well in the process.

Or a school's test scores can dip as a principal takes on the challenges of adopting a rich curriculum and moving away from a "teach to the test" mentality. The value of what happens in a school is in the decisions that the individuals within that school make. The quality of those decisions is then reflected in any number of measures—provided that the measures were properly used.

A policy that places rising test scores as the primary indicator of a school's success is, by definition, indifferent to what is actually taking place in schools. It would be akin to passing a law that required the reported GDP to always be a bit higher than the previous year regardless of the underlying realities, or telling doctors that they had to make a diagnosis regarding blood pressure absent anything but the systolic and diastolic reading provided by a blood pressure cuff.

In all three cases such rules remove the impact of reality, of the context in which things occur, and as a result the numbers are rendered meaningless.

In education, a school can choose to damage its student population by limiting the curriculum to the test and be rewarded exactly the same as one that did right by its students and taught well and richly, rendering the context irrelevant since all that matters are rising test scores. If they move up—absent any evidence of formal cheating—then the policy is satisfied, but the test scores are meaningless.

We have reached this difficult state in education for the simple and worthwhile reason that we care. I have spent my career working with people who advocate for the positions being discussed here, and (almost) every single one of them is a good person doing the best they can to make education everything it can be.

Almost all of them remain convinced that this world of standards and assessments in their current form can and should serve as the basis for schooling, and the issue is with our implementation and execution.

When I present my arguments—as I have here—many of them nod and grant me a number of my points. Many will even admit some agreement with my argument regarding the selection of behavioral standards for education as being a bad one, and virtually all agree that the testing systems in support of them really are just the standardized testing systems of the past with a little more spit and polish on them.

Almost to a tee, however, the conversation will turn to them making a statement something akin to this: John, things were so bad that anything has to be better than what went before. Have you forgotten?

And indeed I have not. In the 1960s and 1970s—and even into the 1980s when I got started in education—I ran into attitudes regarding certain students deemed as "un-teachable" due to the socioeconomic conditions in which they were born, and even in the majority of cases when good teachers reached out to all their students with all their ability the performance data for poor and minority populations showed startling disparities that no one in their right mind would find acceptable.

Similar analysis on school funding, teacher quality, teacher retention, dropout rates, and more showed similar disparities, and what was obvious was that something indeed needed to change.

But the argument that anything is better than nothing when it comes to making changes risks offering a fallacy for a solution. It risks being akin to saying "we needed a needle and thread but you gave us a hammer so at least we have that."

Having the wrong tool is having the wrong tool, and it cannot substitute for the right tool. That they are both tools is true—and useful in their own right against their design—but you can't sew a button with a hammer.

In education, however, all tools seem to be deemed as equal, no matter their design or their purpose, and so long as a policymaker or an education reformer can put something in place the logic seems to be that doing so is sufficient to see great things happen regardless of whether it is the right or the wrong tool.

If it is the wrong tool, those responsible for the tool are simply told to figure it out, to somehow make it fit, to magically transform it into the new, desired thing. That thinking has led to trying to drive our schools with behavioral standards and to measure our success with tools that approximate the status quo, when the design of them both runs counter to the goal of education, and no amount of finagling can make them otherwise.

In no other industry would such inarticulate, shortsighted reasoning be tolerated. In education, we enshrine it in policy, in our public discourse, and worst of all in our schools.

The design of a standardized test is such that it can do one thing, and do that one thing very well, but only under very specific conditions. For too long we have pretended that such tests can do whatever we ask of them, without concern for the conditions under which they are used, and the result is confusion, misunderstanding, and educational stagnation.

When you look at the design underlying such tests, this was predictable and should have been easy to avoid.

Shortsighted—and frankly, frustrated—policymakers applied some bad logic to get to where we are now: if schools that perform at the top end on such tests are representative of the schools we want for our children, then let us get all schools to achieve in similar fashion so that all schools can be like those we admire.

In this chapter I have argued that our obsession with standardized tests scores and a teach-to-the-test mentality is eroding our ability to advance student learning. In the spirit of offering constructive criticism, I need to offer a view of what an alternative might look like—one that a policymaker might be able to embrace. My goal here is to be a pragmatist regarding solutions and not just throw stones at something I don't like or agree with.

Any solution for measuring what happens in education needs to accept that the following questions all demand answers:

1. Did teachers teach what they were supposed to have taught?
2. Did students learn what they were supposed to have learned?
3. What is the consequence of that learning when viewed from a broader perspective?

The single biggest caveat when considering such questions is that not only can no single instrument or measuring device answer all three questions but also no single instrument is capable of answering even a single question. Yet answering all three accurately and fairly is the only way we can understand the degree to which the educational enterprise is or is not working.

What should be immediately obvious is that the distributive paradigm at the heart of standardized tests only apples to the relevance consideration, and then, of course, only if teaching to the test doesn't occur. That runs smack into the reality regarding the actual use of standardized tests, which are used to answer all three questions.

I'll show how the notion of distribution works so that its inability to answer these questions becomes obvious, and then show how we could in fact be answering all three.

The idea that populations distribute around a variety of activities is an extremely important notion in social science research. We chart the distribution of height and weight for each age of a child, airlines need to know the width of people's set of hips so they can build airplane seats that will fit our backsides, and in education, having a sense of which schools with a similar makeup to your own are proving successful in serving as a validation that what they did stands a good chance of working for you.

The purpose of these distributions—as has been discussed—is to give us a snapshot of how things are at a moment in time. Thus, whatever the state of things is at a moment will be reflected in the snapshot, but without judgment. Certainly the distribution in test scores shows the impact of poverty on achievement, the distribution of children's height and weight in a chart helps parents see how their child is growing and progressing, and the distribution of the size of our backsides shows the degree to which they have ticked upward over the past two decades, but any judgments to be made as to a cause are outside the charted distribution of such things.

Because this principle is very important to understand, let's conduct a simple study to see how it works. Let's imagine that we want to know something about the age at which people marry for the first time in a particular state.

We could pick a year and comb through the census and other data sources for the information we needed. Then, once we had that information we could then build a graph in which the horizontal axis included the ages of one to seventy-five (which is a likely estimate for the range of ages for all first marriages in a state in the United States, save for a handful of outliers) and the vertical axis included the number of people at each age that got married, and then populate the graph with the data we had gathered.

It would be reasonable to assume that at the age of one the number of people getting married in our chosen year would be zero—given both common sense and a host of laws and social mores—but then as we moved to the right we would start to see a few getting married in their teenage years, and then the biggest concentration would likely be somewhere in the late twenties or early thirties.

As the age increased, we would likely see fewer and fewer people marrying for the first time, until we reached the age of seventy-five, which we'll assume our imaginary research showed was the maximum age for a first marriage.

The hypothetical graph (see figure 5.1) of state A would show a distributive curve, with lots of clustering around certain ages, and with the curve tapering off at both ends, with a significant tapering after about the age of fifty. In the hypothetical graph I've provided I've intentionally removed the ages from the horizontal axis and the number of people getting married at that age from the vertical axis. I've done so because I want you to think about the shape of a distribution more than anything else—which is why I made up a fictional data set in the first place.

Let's now conduct the exact same study for another state as a point of comparison (see figure 5.2). The second state shows the same basic pattern but with some notable differences. For example, in the second figure a hypo-

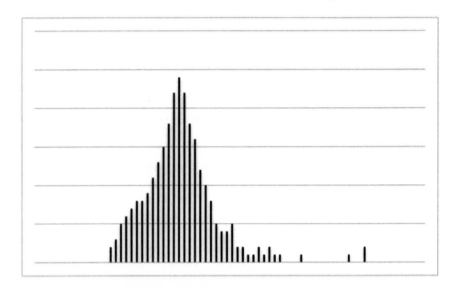

Figure 5.1. **A hypothetical distribution of the age at which people first get married in State A.** *(The horizontal axis represents the ages 1-75, and the vertical axis represents the number of people who married in the hypothetical year being represented.)*

thetical state skews to the right of the original somewhat, indicating that people in this state (theoretically) wait a bit longer before they get married.

We come to understand the nuances of each distribution by applying several tools to the data that help reduce each graph with its thousands of data points to numbers that can be more easily analyzed. We can compute "averages" in several ways, through the mean, the median, and the mode. Mean is the traditional average, median is the midpoint in the data set, and mode is the most commonly occurring point in the data set.

Each is helpful in its own way. Two states could have similar means but arrived at that point via very different routes. One state could have lots of folks getting married at a wide range of ages, and another have lots of folks getting married at a very narrow range of ages, and yet the mean age is the same. To suggest that the two data sets are the same is just dumb—anyone could tell just by looking at the various distributions that they contain differences.

Statisticians calculate how far from the average most of the population falls as a way of understanding how homogenous or diverse each population is when compared to others. They also recognize that any such numbers are always only an estimate. Even if you were extremely vigilant in combing the historical records for marriage data, no one in their right mind would claim

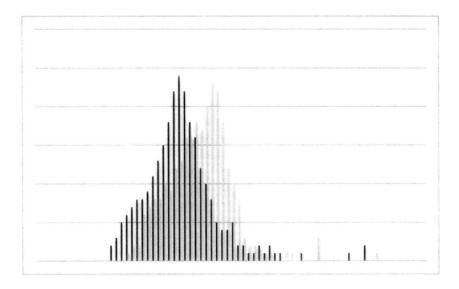

Figure 5.2.   Comparing the distributions of two states.

that your data were 100 percent accurate. Whether through human error, data collection limitations, or a host of other problems and challenges with assembling such a data set, your estimates will have some amount of imprecision in them because you cannot be 100 percent sure that your estimates are 100 percent accurate.

Anyone familiar with a political survey has a sense of this sort of fudge factor—what statisticians call *measurement error*. It is reported for political surveys by saying "plus or minus some percent."

In our study of marriage ages we would find in the end that our data would have some amount of error in it, and we would want to report it so that people don't wrongly interpret what we have done. If the mean age in state A is twenty-five and in state B it is twenty-seven, and the error computes to plus or minus two years, the fact that the difference is within the margin of error means you cannot say that any difference in mean age in the data set truly exists.

You are, in fact, acknowledging that human activity is always a bit imperfect, and that the only appropriate interpretation is to suggest that had you picked a different day to collect the data a reasonable chance exists that B's data would average twenty-five and A's twenty-seven. There is, in this instance, no statistical basis for suggesting that the two averages identify any meaningful differences between the two states.

Now that I have my state-by-state (theoretical) distribution of marriage ages along with a set of statistics that will allow me to compare them in a fair and reasonable manner, I can attempt to answer the question "why?" Why is it that differences exist? Is it because religious or cultural values encourage earlier marriages, or that cold-weather states somehow make people more eager to take the plunge so they have someone to cuddle with, or that beach states exude a culture that eschews responsibility and waits until the last possible moment to say "I do"?

To answer such questions, I have to look at information *outside* the distribution in order to understand what I see in the distribution. Not one of these questions can be answered by looking at the state-by-state distributions or the statistics that describe each data set.

The data sets help inform the types of questions I may want to ask, or it can confirm or refute an earlier hypothesis I may have had, but the answers to the question *why* are completely external to the data set, and to look within it for them would be senseless.

I created my hypothetical example of marriage ages to show very briefly how distributions work because it helps show how education became seduced by such numbers and yet how truly limited they are.

Education was first introduced to the idea that it could be subjected to the distributive paradigm around a hundred years or so ago. A number of psychologists discovered that if they administered tests that consisted of test items that about half the subjects would answer incorrectly that a similar distributive pattern emerged.

These psychologists were searching for a way to quantify intelligence (often for reasons that had to do as much with hubris, blatant racism, and the desire to keep white males at the top of the intellectual food chain—the history of that period is fascinating for its insights into human behavior and the dangers of bad science[4]), and they produced distributions that they claimed identified a mathematical way to do so that you have undoubtedly heard referred to as IQ.[5]

I won't debate here the merits or—as I think most serious scholars now believe—the lack of merit in much of that early work. What is of great significance to the field of education is that one of those early psychologists, Lewis Terman, while at Stanford University gave us the first edition of the Stanford Achievement Test, which was based upon this distributive principle.

Terman's intent was to sell his test to schools for the purpose of identifying "giftedness" in students (another term that is fraught with all sorts of baggage) so that they could be culled out from the masses and educated separately. The test proved to be very popular, and in its wake it spawned a number of other standardized test series, until I took a version of the Stanford as part of my schooling and worked on a later version of it in my professional career.

By the time I was in school, the tests had evolved to the point that they had become almost entirely subject based and the statistical sophistication was such that the bias in the earlier editions had been removed. And they, of course, used scanning technology, which enabled us to bubble in our responses with that ubiquitous #2 pencil. I've already discussed testing's evolution to our current spate of tests, so I won't rehash that.

(I will note one thing, however. One of the really interesting rhetorical tricks we have played on ourselves was to accept the label of "achievement tests" for these instruments. It is true that as a proxy for achievement—as an estimate that could offer a comparison of responses between schools—they worked rather well.

But to say that they accurately and precisely measured what was achieved in schools is absolutely not true, nor would they make that claim. The items were not selected for that purpose, the statistical design itself has a very different function, and the overall purpose was to offer comparisons, not grade anyone's performance. "Achievement test" referenced the proxy target, but it may also serve as the misnomer that made people think these instruments may directly measure the thing called achievement.)

Whether your distribution is determined by gathering census data regarding the age at which people get married or a set of test items designed to show a distribution, to look into a distribution and attempt to ascertain a cause is, as I said, senseless. The difference is that in the case of census data the nature of the data won't even allow for that sort of look.

But in the case of a test, the fact that the test content looks and feels like something we can relate to creates a temptation that is hard to resist—so tempting that our policies now insist that we do just that, and in response nearly every school in this country follows suit, despite the utter inappropriateness in doing so.

The test items serve as a data-gathering resource, exactly like a census record indicating a marriage age. To treat them as anything else is inappropriate.

With a sense of the limits of the distributive paradigm and the resulting distributions, let's return now to the three questions we need answered if our assessment of a school or a classroom is to be complete:

1. Did a teacher teach what they were supposed to have taught?
2. Did a student learn what they were supposed to have learned?
3. What is the consequence of that learning when viewed from a broader perspective?

In the reform environment, what was attempted—and is still being attempted—is to carry forth the idea that all children could and should learn at very high levels, along with the acknowledgment that every child is different and that those differences will manifest themselves in terms of learning patterns, the time to complete activities, and the age at which complex material can be properly grasped.

Under that aegis, what is so educationally significant about the fact that as of a date certain children can be shown to distribute across a broad spectrum in terms of achievement? What does that have to do with the delivery of a curriculum, student success at learning the material, or the success of a school at ensuring that every child has a chance?

The answer is not much.

When the only question you ask and answer is "how do my students rank against each other," that is the only question you can answer. If the tool is asked to answer a question for which it was not designed you will, to repeat my metaphor, have selected the wrong tool for the job.

Which is precisely what we have done. We selected a single tool based upon a paradigm well outside the goals of the reform movement that doesn't do any of the things assigned to it by policymakers and expect it to work nonetheless.

It cannot.

The right tool to answer question #1 regarding the quality of teaching needs to answer all of the questions we have for what a good teacher is: are they current in their application of practice, do they differentiate instruction to accommodate the unique needs of their students, do they deliver the assigned curriculum in a manner that is engaging to students?

The following are three simple examples of the kinds of tools that could be used in making such determination that are in fact designed to do so:

1. Rich *fulfillment* standards regarding professional development, peer tutoring, and continuing education.
2. A system of short quizzes to be administered at the *end* of a class or a lesson directly concerning what was intended to be taught—the quizzes would be scored and used by a teacher to show how effectively they taught the lesson, where shortcomings occurred, and what might need to be retaught and to whom.
3. A rich peer review system—one that requires teachers to regularly watch and rate a few minutes of each teacher in action—that can then aggregate the responses for use by a teacher to guide and adjust practice.

None of these, perhaps not surprisingly, rank order teachers or has anything to do with distributions. All can be carefully monitored for compliance, and all have to do with ensuring the appropriateness of the delivered curriculum.

Answering question #2, did a student learn what they were supposed to have learned, could be accomplished by a number of avenues, but here we start to move out of the traditional stand and deliver models of instruction in which all students are expected to learn at a similar pace and in a similar way.

An example of this comes from my own experience: after a year of teaching university-level writing as a graduate student, I suspected I wasn't really a very good teacher. The fact was that the students who entered my class as good writers left as good writers, and those who struggled as writers at the beginning of the semester were just as likely to struggle at the end.

I don't mean to suggest that the students didn't get anything out of my classes, but I was deeply bothered by the fact that most of them left without me accomplishing what I thought a writing teacher was supposed to do, which was to help everyone write well.

During my first summer break I read something by Peter Elbow that told of an experiment he conducted wherein he walked into class with no syllabus, told the students that they weren't leaving until they had each written well, and they were off.[6] I wasn't then at a small liberal arts college working in a system that didn't assign grades as was Elbow, so I built his idea into a syllabus that was short, sweet, and to the point: write well once for a C, a few times more for a B, and a few times more than that for an A.

The grade was theirs for the choosing and would be determined only by the amount of effort they were willing to put into the class and their work. Once a student had earned a C so long as they did the seat time (a requirement at the time) they had their C: if that happened the first week of school that was fine by me.

Following the first round of papers, I could again tell who was or was not a good writer, but what was remarkable was that I could not predict the grade anyone would eventually earn. In the end, I had some good writers that took a B or a C and put their efforts elsewhere, and I had some fairly poor writers who put in the time and the effort to earn an A. The traditional distribution of high achievers down to low achievers with the grades similarly apportioned did not apply.

But what really struck me were the numbers of students that came to me and indicated that this was the first time they had ever truly succeeded at something, that up to that point they had survived on B-level work (or in a few instances, even worse than that) and the world somehow seemed satisfied, so they had never bothered to try harder. Some of my most challenged students indicated that it was the first time anyone had ever expected that level of performance from them, and so it was the first time they had ever given it.

Extend that thinking to the entire school population, and it is perhaps the most damning evidence that we have that our behavioral standards as the basis for what a student should learn aren't working: the vast majority of students still walk away from school without having performed at a level of excellence that I believe is the right of every student.

That was my first experience with a fulfillment standard, and it showed me the power of such a standard properly placed. It made the fulfillment of a precise standard the only acceptable goal, removing time as the variable and replacing it with effort.

Fulfillment standards that can drive student behavior in a manner we would all want are not difficult to imagine. For example, I mentioned several in the chapter regarding standards:

- Successful participation in three or more Advanced Placement or International Baccalaureate courses
- Accurate completion of 80 percent of the stretch goals included with weekly mathematics assignments
- Successful participation in planning and carrying out three out of the five annual academic service projects
- All students will read at a fluency rate of x words per minute by x grade
- All students will produce a well-executed piece of writing once each year without time as the constraint
- All students will complete a complex analysis involving mathematical concepts in each year of schooling, without time as the constraint
- In order to graduate, do one of the following:

  1. Conduct a short play and put it on outside regular school hours
  2. Put on an art exhibition displaying no fewer than six original pieces created by the student
  3. Perform for an audience of not fewer than twenty—alone or with one to three other students—three or more works of music by a known artist or composer

- Each student that matriculates from one grade cluster to the next will have taught a mathematical concept to a small group of younger students, assigned and corrected their homework, and worked with the students to correct misunderstandings
- Students that double the number of graduation standards met will earn an honorary diploma
- Advanced Placement Diploma
- International Baccalaureate Diploma

Each of these—and any fulfillment standard you could come up with—involves a deep understanding of content, requires a great deal of effort, and accepts only a successful performance in compliance with the requirement.

When students meet the requirement they will have done something that can be recognized by the teachers, their peers, and the community as worthwhile.

Teachers who work with students as they attempt to comply with such standards will have to deploy a wide range of resources in order to do so that involve far more content than in any current state standards document, that tap the skills students need to learn and develop in order to survive in the world beyond school, and that, are frankly, good for kids to learn.

As to timing on the standards, like my students in the writing class, no one need be asked to reach the same level of proficiency on a standardized test in lockstep with all the other students by some date certain, because time and effort for a student to comply would differ. Accountability in such an environment could be about getting students to that level of proficiency, with particular attention being given to schools and students for whom compliance is a real struggle.

But student learning is also measurable through a good old-fashioned exam, based on the curriculum that was actually delivered, without regard for its distributive properties. A good essay exam is one that replaces a conversation a teacher would have with a student to determine mastery of the material but that for the sake of time and efficiency cannot be had directly. Students would have to demonstrate their learning and provide direct evidence of it. If students were taught *The Great Gatsby* during a course, they deserve to see questions about *The Great Gatsby* on the test—not generic, multiple-choice items that are easy to score or are designed for use on a standardized test.

Such exams should not be constructed to allow a set of adults to evaluate the nuances among various populations of students but allow students to show the degree to which they had mastered the assigned material. They should be based on a design in which all students can earn every possible point and not on one where that would actually invalidate the measure.

And teaching to them? Absolutely fine. Do it. The items would be based on the curriculum and only once that curriculum was mastered could they be answered. Teaching in anticipation of such exams wouldn't invalidate anything.

As a check on the system, we also need to answer the last question in the list: what is the consequence of what was learned when viewed from a broader perspective? Once a student has learned something, we need to understand its broader relevance: is it in check with what others throughout the country are doing? Are the fulfillment standards being applied similarly to others? Is acceptable writing in one part of the country similar to acceptable writing in another?

When I started my work in education many years ago, the project I was assigned was one that attempted just this sort of definition.[7] At the time, however, email was still a bit of a novelty and the future power of the

Internet was suspected but not yet realized. Still, what we quickly realized was that to establish anything approaching a universal "good enough" distinction required lots of examples of student work, compiled into massive databases, and made available in a whole variety of forms and formats so that the distinction could be similarly understood and applied. We lacked the technological know-how to do it.

Twenty years later the know-how exists. It is not much of an intellectual challenge anymore to conceptualize the systems that would be required to standardize each outcome so that a student meeting a standard in one place can be declared to have accomplished the same thing as a student who did it in another. Evidence could be compiled within such systems that the quality required in the standard could be made clear, and the policy and educational worlds could then come together to finally decide if the standards were high enough, and if not, raise them in a manner everyone can understand.

Answering the question regarding the consequence of what was learned would be the one place in which a proxy such as a standardized test *might* be useful—but *only* if the system is such that no one would ever think of using it as the basis for instruction. The one thing standardized tests do very well—because it is what they were designed to do and it is all that they were designed to do—is offer up a basis of comparison through which each school and student can see themselves.

Properly managed, such a test could serve as one of several indicators as to whether or not what students were learning was in line with the rest of the country.

I would be careful with this as an accountability choice, however, as our history with such instruments is one of highly inappropriate use. I would prefer some of the instruments mentioned in the last few pages, because when—not if—policymakers get a hold of them and attempt to put them into law good things can still happen as a result.

As long as a proxy is in place in a similar role, the risk exists that the proxy will replace the things that actually matter. It did once before, and given the chance it is likely to happen once again.

At the beginning of this section I suggested that three broad educational formulas were currently at play. The first, the generic formula, went like this:

Expectations for Students

+

Good Teaching

+

Evidence of Success

=

Academically Prepared Students

Educational reformers then put their own spin on it, with the goal being for it to look something like this:

Rich, Common Expectations for Students
+
Great Teaching
+
Success on Assessments That Require Students to Demonstrate Those Expectations
=
Academically Prepared Students

I then suggested that the practical, unintended reality is much closer to this:

State Content Standards in Reading and Math
+
Teaching Focused on Tested Content
+
Success on Standardized Tests
=
Students That Are Pretty Good at Taking Tests

I hope now that you understand why I believe the last formula dominates the educational landscape even though those responsible for the current form of the educational reform movement put a very different spin on it that resembles the second.

Our current system of standards uses behavioral standards as the model and then asks those behavioral standards to do a task for which they are ill prepared. Our schools are now required by policy to adjust their teaching as a result of standardized test scores, which were built for an entirely different purpose.

What should be a curriculum-independent measure, akin to a census record or a data collection tool, is now presumed to be the primary arbiter of curriculum change.

Now, with the introduction of the Common Core standards and assessments, those responsible for those activities are working from the assumption that we got the formula right but somehow missed on the standards and assessments. But they, too, have selected behavioral standards as the model for the standards and the distributive testing paradigm for the assessments.

The new standards and assessments offer some new and improved twists to an old structure that remains inadequate for the accountability task. The last formula that implies that success on standardized tests is the goal of education, however, is still very much in play.

NOTES

1. John R. Tanner, "Missing the Mark: What Test Scores Really Tell Us," *School Administrator* 68, no. 9 (2011): 14.

2. U.S. National Archives and Records Administration, *Code of Federal Regulations*, Improving the Academic Achievement of the Disadvantaged; Final Rule, Title 1, sec. 200.5.

3. For example, the technical reports for Virginia can be accessed at http://www.doe.virginia.gov/testing/test_administration/index.shtml#technical_reports, and the reports for Massachusetts can be accessed at http://www.doe.mass.edu/mcas/tech/.

4. Steven Jay Gould, *The Mismeasure of Man* (New York: W. W. Norton and Company, 1996), 185–204.

5. A great many scholars, researchers, and writers have been able to show just how sketchy the idea of innate intelligence is. This has in no way prevented it from permeating popular culture, but it is now beyond doubt that the principles these early scholars advocated for: that intelligence is innate, that it is permanent and unchanging, and that your level of intelligence should be the basis for determining what type of future you should be entitled to have been completely and utterly debunked. An excellent example of this is in Stephen Jay Gould's critique of "The Bell Curve," included as the last chapter in his revised edition of *The Mismeasure of Man*.

6. The idea comes from an article by Peter Elbow that I can no longer locate. Elbow is the author of *Writing without Teachers*, in which he also advocates some of the ideas I reference here.

7. The New Standards Project was run jointly by both the National Center for Education and the Economy, and the Learning, Research, and Development Center at the University of Pittsburgh. It represented one of the early attempts to define the levels of performance for what actually constituted meeting a standard.

II

Accountability

When a building falls down or a bridge fails, we examine everything we can discover about anything even remotely related to the processes of designing, building, inspecting, and maintaining the structure.

Education deserves the same courtesy. Failure of a structure like a building or a bridge does not automatically presuppose the fault, and yet failure in schools for the past few decades has been automatically presumed to be the fault of teachers.

Lots of policymakers may object to such a generalization, but the one constant that seems to emerge from every recent policy conversation is to tie state test scores in reading and math to teachers, as if that will identify who is to blame when things don't work out the way we hoped.

What is most unique about the systems that make up the structure of our reforms is that they function as an exoskeleton that constrains what happens in our schools to the point that the true goals of education are actually outside and beyond those constraints.

Accountability is the mantra under which those constraints are imposed. What is left is an unworkable system, one that demands schools operate within those constraints while insisting they produce a result that is, in the end, clearly outside of them.

Chapter Six

Accountability within the Educational Formula

Much of what I have tried to do so far is to show how we might move closer to the educational formula most reformers think we actually have in place by showing the gaps between what was in fact done versus what was intended. Now I need to dig a bit deeper into what currently exists.

It is one thing to show that the system isn't what people thought they were creating and quite another thing to show the shortcomings of what was actually created. If I don't do this then the argument can still be made that at least what we have is better than nothing, and that is not a point I'm willing to concede.

I'm going to limit my focus in this chapter to the success determination in the educational formula, which is now largely given over to standardized tests. I'll focus on what I see to be five major shortcomings in the current incantation of the formula, focusing on the nature of how the decision regarding success is made.

The five shortcomings are as follows:

1. Single point-in-time judgments are notoriously unreliable absent additional instruments.
2. Point in time (synchronic) judgments offer a very limited basis for judging anything.
3. One-third of the faculty or only a part of the curriculum now carries the burden for the quality decision in a school.
4. Good teaching is not required for the system to work.
5. The goal of the intended formula is outside the educational formula as implemented.

SINGLE POINT-IN-TIME JUDGMENTS ARE NOTORIOUSLY
UNRELIABLE

What would happen if a doctor used only a single instrument to make a diagnosis about a patient?

A stethoscope that finds a regular heartbeat and lungs free of pneumonia is incapable of offering up an opinion when it comes to diabetes, for which the proper tool would be a glucose test.

A blood pressure cuff can say a great deal about whether or not someone has high blood pressure, but it says nothing about whether or not a patient needs an antibiotic to treat an infection. And so it goes. Should any one instrument be brought forward and be presented as the only instrument a doctor should use, the results would be catastrophic. Patients that are unhealthy would be deemed to be just fine. Patients identified through the instrument as needing attention would be at the mercy of an uninformed opinion as to what to do next, resulting in massive inefficiency and less-than-stellar outcomes.

Even worse, when an intervention works it will not be because it was selected as the best intervention given the overall needs of the patient, but because someone made a lucky guess. Think of the old adage regarding test taking that when you don't know the answer just mark C. The reason is pretty simple: assuming four choices, if you always chose C odds are 25 percent of your C responses would in fact land on the correct answers, since most tests randomize the response pattern. The point is that if you guess consistently you stand a chance of hitting on the right answer often enough that you might fool somebody into thinking it's something other than luck if they only bothered to look at the correct responses.

Or consider a second adage: a broken clock tells the correct time twice a day. If the clock was frozen at 6:00 and you happened to glance at it twice that day, once at 6:00 a.m. and once at 6:00 p.m., you might indeed think that the clock was accurate and doing its job. In fact, you could act on what you perceived as being accurate information, and due to the fact that you happened to look at just the right time your actions would be seen as successful *because* of the clock even though the clock had nothing to do with it. A single-instrument system cannot, by definition, work. When it appears to, it is either because we guessed consistently over time and as a result hit on the right answer at least some of the time, or we got lucky in that our actions were right even though the instrument readings were in fact unrelated to the selected action. Some remarkable things happen the instant a second instrument can be added to the mix. For example, the result of the first instrument can be seen as incomplete, as when a stethoscope alone shows a person's heartbeat and lungs to be healthy while a glucose test suggests that diabetes is just around the corner.

Or an outcome can be shown to be the result of lucky guessing and not a good decision-making process, which is what happens with an old-fashioned curative: if you took it for every possible ailment eventually one day you just might have the ailment it was designed to cure. On that day it would work.

Additional information would go a long way toward matching the right cure for what ails you.

Or—and this is important in the conversation here—an instrument can be shown to be flawed or even broken. A second watch that can actually tell time can call into question the one that cannot. If the first instrument gives a bad reading, the addition of additional instruments and additional readings can show it as an outlier and subject the reading to additional scrutiny.

The probability of a bad judgment being made from a single instrument is huge. The probability of a bad judgment by an instrument that wasn't designed to judge the quality of anything in the first place is even higher, placing our use of standardized testing on pretty precarious ground.

We are, of course, trapped in a paradigm in education that accepts and even celebrates high-stakes testing as a single-instrument system in spite of a rather significant number of warnings against such a thing, most prominently in the standards for testing published by the American Psychological Association, the American Educational Research Association, and the National Council on Measurement in Education and relied on by the industry as the guide for what is or is not appropriate.[1]

We rely on standardized testing as that single instrument, and while it appears in a number of forms (e.g., end-of-year tests, end-of-course tests, many formative assessments), they are all based upon a similar set of assumptions: that seeing the distribution of students—which was never designed to make an educational quality determination—says just about everything there is to know about educational quality.

Jim Popham, a well-respected writer on this subject, declares doing so akin to "measuring temperature with a teaspoon."[2]

SYNCHRONIC JUDGMENTS OFFER A VERY LIMITED BASIS FOR JUDGING ANYTHING

In putting forth that single indicator of quality, we have forgotten all sorts of incredibly important rules for how one makes a decision in life: most importantly, that the greatest lessons come from understanding things from a historical perspective, and then working hard not to make the mistakes of the past as well as learn from our successes.

Historians work from the assumption that there are two ways to view the past: synchronically and diachronically. These are really just fancy words for a view that represents a single slice of time (synchronic) versus events over time (diachronic). The combination of both provides a picture of the past that makes it much easier to understand what happened and where lessons can be learned.

For example, if I want to really understand what happened to bring about some historical situation, I really need multiple perspectives. On the one hand, I need to understand the sequence of events that led to the situation, what the motives were of people making the decisions, and the information on which those decisions were based. I need to know something—most importantly from this perspective—about cause and effect so I can get at answers to the question, why?

But in order to do that I also need to understand what that moment in time looked like. I need to know what the prevailing attitudes were toward such things as of that moment, and I need to know what dynamics existed that might have influenced an outcome in order to better understand and make sense of the situation and determine how that differs from the present.

Absent either view, the picture is incomplete. If all I have are the causal connections—that is, this happened, then as a result that happened—I can study those things, but I risk doing so in a vacuum, and any conclusions won't offer any advice or insights to those of us reading the history and attempting to learn from it.

If all I have is insight into a slice of time, I'm missing any sense of how we may have arrived at that moment, and thus any inferences I make will be little more than conjecture.

Note that when a doctor attempts to work with a patient a similar dynamic applies: the doctor will look at a patient's history and symptoms (the diachronic perspective) and then order up a host of bloodwork and other tests (the synchronic perspective) to see what interpretations can be made once the two perspectives can be viewed side by side.

Again, with only one perspective you risk being terribly wrong: the patient history may include hints of a variety of problems that can only be narrowed by the tests, or without the tests the doctor will have to guess at the condition of the patient.

Standardized tests in reading and mathematics are a synchronic measure—and a particularly narrow one at that. They are administered as of a date certain each year, are designed to show a synchronic distribution of students on that date, and they offer zero comment as to how they came to be.

They were not designed to comment about educational quality, about the quality of teaching that produced them, or about the nature of the school experience that somehow ranked students in the order that it did. And in the current accountability package, the tests are limited to two school subjects—

important subjects, of course, that are foundational to the learning process—but still just a part of the overall system.

Nowhere in the accountability package do we have a diachronic component—the piece about what happens over time. Even in situations in which multiple synchronic measures are taken throughout the year (in simpler terms that would be a version of a standardized test that would be administered multiple times throughout the year—several states already do this and more are preparing to do so as of this writing), the diachronic piece is still missing because we lack that causal story as an explicit part of the accountability package.

Every decision that occurs in a school happens outside that synchronic moment in time, and yet those decisions deserve to be a part of the package if actual accountability is the goal. That would mean that schools need to be held accountable for their decisions: "In our school we worked on x and y and expected to see the following things occur, and here is the evidence that they did or did not."

It is incredibly ironic to me that we claim to hold schools accountable for the decisions they make and yet don't include those decisions anywhere in the package. Instead, we allow the synchronic approach to carry the full weight of judgment without regard to the decisions.

Studying history under such conditions would be useless, and practicing medicine would be just plain dangerous. In education, it leaves us blind as to which decisions were good ones and which decisions were bad, leaving us to guess. That means that success will be very difficult to scale, and our reasons for failure will be very difficult to identify and fix.

Inefficiency and frustration are predictable outcomes.

The outcomes for students are incredibly important, of course, but even if the test results weren't the result of a teach to-the-test mentality a distribution of how students rank is still of limited value in understanding such outcomes.

But let's go even further and suggest just for a moment that on this point I may be dead wrong: that how students rank is capable of serving as an effective proxy for determining the quality of an outcome.

Even if that were the case, absent the decisions that led to those outcomes we would still only have a partial picture, along with all of the risks that come with attempting to understand the outcome without a full understanding of which decisions led to the perceived effect.

CARRYING THE BURDEN FOR THE QUALITY DECISION IN A SCHOOL

The concern here can be stated very concisely: no system can be declared fair when a significant number of people in a building are held accountable for what happens that is beyond their control. I can be a PE teacher or a coach and encourage academics—even require them for students to participate in the case of a coach—but the actual lessons are up to others.

If I'm a science teacher I certainly can and should make grammar count in my student's papers, but my job is to teach science, and I need to stay focused on doing that well—the grammar lessons are someone else's job.

Even if I want to make the argument that mathematics and reading are the job of everyone, not everyone has been trained to teach reading and mathematics. Just because you and I can read and do math in no way qualifies us to teach it.

And yet in schools we assign two subjects and some subset of the faculty to carry the full weight of accountability for the school and presume that doing so is appropriate.

GOOD TEACHING NOT REQUIRED

In the chapter on test scores I pointed out that if all you care about is nudging test scores upward you stand a pretty good chance of being able do that with a teach-to-the-test mentality. Of course, that risks damaging a student's long-term chances for success and invalidates the test scores, but at the same time it helps preserve the school as an intact institution, which is ultimately what the current accountability package offers as the goal.

In other words, the practical effect of making a test score the arbiter of school quality is that good teaching is desirable but not necessary for moving test scores forward.

Perhaps the thinking was that our teaching force is so bad and so poorly trained that we had to have a system that could work in spite of them, or that we so despise the preservice training that teachers receive when earning their degrees that we want to make it irrelevant by creating a system in which it doesn't matter. I'm being cynical here, but I don't think I'm far from the truth.

For as long as I have been engaged in the educational enterprise teachers have suffered an inordinate amount of criticism. I can think of any number of articles that attempted to work through the historical and sociological reasons why this was so, and while many offered a compelling story, they failed to turn the tide of public opinion.

The result—as I have mentioned already—is that teachers under the reform mantra have been effectively removed as the arbiter of educational quality and have been replaced with test scores, which by design cannot comment upon educational quality. That has to be seen as a real slap in the face to the profession, not to mention illogical.

Not only were teachers removed from that role but also they have now been told that the skills that are most desirable are those that can help test scores trend upward, which, for the umpteenth time, can be made to happen—or at least attempted—via very bad teaching. Bad teaching, it seems, is an acceptable norm in education, and the goal of reform is to inoculate the system so that it doesn't affect the kids.

That hardly seems to me a productive starting point in the conversation for how to make education great.

I am not suggesting that all of the perceptions toward those in the teaching profession are entirely unwarranted. I do believe that the profession has for some time been in need of a reboot, and that for too long we have accepted a degraded professional standing (that is different, of course, from a degraded profession—one has to do with a perception, and one with the profession itself—I'm speaking only of the perception) as the norm.

I believe it imperative that we reprofessionalize teaching so that it becomes a desirable career choice for which students compete the same way they do in other fields, as well as show our appreciation for those in it who have made teaching their career choice.

What I do not believe—and never will—is that the decision to remove teachers as the arbiter of quality was a good one. If teachers were accepting mediocre work, that problem should have been addressed directly. If bad teachers were slipping through the tenure process, that problem should have been addressed directly. If teacher training was the problem, then that, too, should have been addressed directly.

Instead, the solution was one that seemed to throw its hands in the air, accept the erroneous assumption that we were stuck with a middling group of people who chose the teaching profession as a last resort for a career and can never learn or get better, and now must impose upon them systems that can work in spite of their mediocrity.

At the same time, the expectation is that in spite of those constraints it is still every teacher's job to provide a vibrant, dynamic education that accounts for the individual needs of every student.

The problem is that as long as teachers are constrained to pseudoprofessional status, the system is likely to continue to produce a pseudoacceptable result. To believe anything else is to believe in the magic of transmogrification such that a system designed under one set of assumptions and constraints can produce results entirely outside and beyond those assumptions and constraints.

Remember that the decisions that lead to a set of test scores are part of the diachronic view of things that is excluded from the accountability package. As long as that view is excluded, the system can be said to not be concerned with what those decisions are, or whether they actually take into consideration the long-term well-being of the students and the profession.

THE GOAL IS OUTSIDE THE FORMULA AS IMPLEMENTED

The stated goal of the accountability package is pretty clear: well-educated students who are ready to advance into the worlds of college and work.

Defining what this looks like has turned into a cottage industry over the last ten years, with some focusing on the specific skill sets students will need, others on the amount of content or knowledge such that students can be considered to be "educated," and still others looking for evidence that can serve as a "readiness" signal for promotion, graduation, or college/workplace readiness.

The stated goal of the current accountability package is located outside or beyond the accountability package as currently deployed. Consider the following realities:

1. Standardized tests are not designed to measure skills. For example, skill sets such as being able to solve complex, multistep problems, being able to extend what was learned in one field to another, or the ability to persevere through a long, tough process are critical to long-term success but are not generally a part of the standard testing universe. The reason for this is simple—students learn and express such skills in a manner that is anything but predictable, and as such items that attempt to go after such skills fail to behave against the required patterns needed for identifying a distribution of students. Complex skills from a measurement perspective tend to be very messy compared to simple content, and so if the idea is to produce a distributive measure it just makes sense to go with the content best suited for that purpose. That means, however, that some of the larger purposes of schooling tend to be well outside the accountability package imposed on schools, since that package is based on standardized test scores.

2. It would be very tricky for all students to achieve at or above a passing score on a standardized test. The nature of the tests is such that unless items contribute to a distribution they would be eliminated from consideration for inclusion. Thus a requirement or even a desire that all students would perform well on a standardized test runs counter to what a standardized test is designed to do. Having selected a standard-

ized test as the primary measurement tool means that all does in fact not really mean all. We can pretend it does, which our policies do, but if that were really the case for accountability purposes, the distributive paradigm was the wrong basis for determining success.

3. There is no such thing as a readiness signal regarding, say, readiness for the world of work, college, or grade promotion on a standardized test of reading or mathematics. It does not, cannot, and will never exist. The closest you can come is to analyze the outcomes of students scoring at each point to see what their future performance looked like, which would likely show a general trend in that the better students performed on a standardized test the more likely they would be to experience long-term success. However, a similar type of conclusion would be reached by looking at the socioeconomic status of the test takers, since that socioeconomic status is likely to be reflected in the distribution. A readiness signal on tests of limited content, then, risks being one more claim that the secret sauce to success is being raised in the right zip code, which as a notion is something that education reform does not (and should not) believe in. The evidence is to the contrary—schools can trump socioeconomic status, but a readiness determination based on the present socioeconomic status risks pre-serving that socioeconomic status (I'll deal with this at length in a later chapter).

4. Much of the information a student needs to succeed in college and the world of work is not a part of schooling. David Conley's work has been instrumental in making this point in terms of both content and the manner in which one goes about selecting and applying to a college or university. Selecting and applying are themselves skills and represent a literacy of sorts that not all students have access to.[3] Studies are clear that students from lower socioeconomic backgrounds are blessed with less information than is necessary in order to make such deci-sions, and yet when that information is provided their ability to get into a school that maximizes their future opportunities is commensu-rate with their wealthier peers.[4] If college and career readiness is a goal of education, that must include ensuring that students understand and have the opportunity to take advantage of such a thing, which is well beyond any reading or math score.

The bottom line is that a slice-in-time measure has zero capacity to look back and determine its cause, or to look forward and predict a future. It can, at best, suggest where one might begin the search for causality, but that is it. A single slice-in-time measure, then, operates outside the goals of the reform movement.

The value of an education needs to be seen in terms of what it can do for the student long term, rendering test scores in reading and math a limited means by which to offer comment regarding that future.

The educational formula that was desired under the umbrella of education reform is one that could say a great deal about how effectively students had been prepared to face the worlds of college and work, could comment upon the effectiveness of teachers and schools, and could do so in a believable manner.

Our selection of a limited point-in-time measure based on content in two subject areas and designed to help us understand a rank ordering of students leaves us a long way from answering any of those questions well.

NOTES

1. American Educational Research Association, *Standards for Educational and Psychological Testing* (Washington, DC: American Educational Research Association, American Psychological Association, and the National Council on Measurement in Education, 1999), 163.

2. W. James Popham, "Why Standardized Tests Don't Measure Educational Quality," *Educational Leadership* 56, no. 6 (1999): 9.

3. David T. Conley, *College and Career Ready: Helping All Students Succeed Beyond High School* (San Francisco: Jossey-Bass, 2010), 48–52.

4. David Leonhardt, "A Simple Way to Send Poor Kids to Top Colleges," *New York Times*, March 29, 2013. http://www.nytimes.com/2013/03/31/opinion/sunday/a-simple-way-to-send-poor-kids-to-top-colleges.html?hp&_r=3&, accessed April 10, 2013.

Chapter Seven

The Bigger Idea of School Accountability

Insisting that schools be held accountable for educating our children is a no-brainer. We entrust schools with the most precious resource we have as parents, we invest a significant amount of money in the process, and we have every right to know that schools are intent on keeping up their end of the bargain.

The challenge is in knowing what it looks like.

For example, someone needs to be accountable for properly funding education, for ensuring the teachers are properly trained, for ensuring that they have the necessary materials to do their jobs well, for ensuring that they teach what they are assigned to teach, and that students learn what they are assigned to learn.

Someone needs to ensure that teachers are properly compensated for their efforts.

Someone needs to ensure that each school has what it needs to properly see to the unique needs of its students, that principals are well trained as managers and leaders, that students are safe, that they are fed—when that isn't something that can happen at home—and that they all get a shot at college or a decent job.

Someone needs to be held accountable for paying particular attention to students with special needs, to those learning English, and to those students that are most at risk for dropping out.

And since no two schools are the same, someone needs to see to it that each school is putting all of this together in an optimal manner such that the combination of the available resources, the constraints that are a necessary part of any job, and the day-to-day work of school staff serves to maximize the benefits of schooling for the maximum number of children given the unique nature of the school.

The metaphor that best describes how we actually decide all of the above at present is a figure of speech called *synecdoche* that some of you may remember from your English classes. *Synecdoche* is a part of something that comes to stand for the whole, as when someone says, "Give me a hand," and what is meant isn't just "a hand" but all of the person attached to that hand.

As a figure of speech it is incredibly common: "lend me your ear" refers to much more than just an ear, a "breadwinner" usually brings home other things as well, and giving your heart to a loved one is far more appreciated when it is accompanied by the rest of you.

In schools, reading and mathematics standardized test scores now act as a stand-in for everything I included in the list of accountabilities above and then some. Reading and math are incredibly important subjects, of course, but the question must be asked: Are standardized test scores in those subjects—especially given the penchant in schools to make them the basis for instruction, undermining their ability to do what they were designed to do, which is not to make a judgment regarding educational quality—capable of standing in for all of those other accountabilities?

Even if the test scores are legitimate, are they even related to some of them?

And wouldn't it be true that an accountability failure in funding or training opportunities or another area that can hurt the reading and mathematics test scores should serve as a precursor to looking at reading and math scores so that each accountability measure can be properly meted?

And what about everything else that happens in a school? At best, reading and math take up a third to half the instructional effort depending on the grade, and lots of schools have lots of employees that don't work in classrooms where reading and math are taught.

If schools were a business, I don't believe we would tolerate this.

A company that focused only on revenue and not on expenses would bankrupt itself in no time flat—revenue is, of course, critical, but so, too, is ensuring that the expenses are kept in check so that the company can make a profit. A carpenter can turn dozens of table legs on a lathe, but until he also builds the tabletops he can't assemble a table. And so it goes.

For some reason we don't seem to mind asking for a different logic to apply to schools. So reading and mathematics test scores it is. They stand in as a tiny part of a gigantic whole and offer themselves as the basis by which the entire thing will be judged.

On the one hand, unraveling school accountability as it currently stands is pretty straightforward: if reading and mathematics scores are trending upward, then a school avoids sanctions. If they are not, then over time a series of more and more draconian sanctions are applied until at some point the state is required to replace school staff with others capable of changing the direction of those scores.

The tests weren't designed for that purpose, and our standards are nowhere as precise as they need to be to actually drive the types of behavior we want to see in our schools, so odds are it won't work. Case closed.

My goal in this book, however, is to unravel the mystery in such things. When it comes to school accountability, that means we need to understand why it was so important, what it was trying to do, and how it took its current form. Only then are we in a position to consider something different.

The notions behind a school accountability package come via models offered by the business community. The purpose of a business accountability package is to motivate behaviors that are good for the organization as well as offer value to those the organization serves.

Now—a caveat here. Motivating the proper behaviors is what an accountability package is supposed to do. I would be remiss not to point out that the model often fails in business. Enron, WorldCom, and the subprime mortgage mess are just three examples in which the failures were obvious, and anyone who has worked for multiple organizations I'm sure has seen a range of quality in terms of how each organization managed the process.

We are going to talk about intent, however, and in that vein I ask for your indulgence.

An accountability package consists of the formal programs organizations put in place to evaluate their employees, most generally on an annual basis, as well as informally through any number of feedback mechanisms that are just a part of the process of people doing their work. Getting the assignments you want, face time with the boss, and public praise (or the lack of any of them) help show an employee how their work is being valued throughout the year as the work is actually being done, and they serve the purposes of accountability as much as a formal once-a-year event.

A successful accountability package is as much about creating a culture in an organization as anything else, and to be honest, much more value comes to the organization in this regard through the informal than the formal components of the package.

I've worked at some good companies that treated the annual accountability event as little more than a perfunctory gesture, and some that made it into a monumental, multistep undertaking that resulted in pages and pages of feedback and documentation. In both cases I learned much more about the type of culture the company was trying to form from the informal processes than from the formal.

Regardless of how any business handles its formal and informal accountability components, all companies are in business to turn a profit, and whether or not they do is the primary indicator of success.

It doesn't matter whether you are a tobacco company, an organic apple farmer, a publisher of children's books, or a dance troupe, they all share this single profit metric because it has the power to capture and coalesce everything that happens within an organization over a year into a single number that everyone, regardless of background, training, or the industry in which they work, can understand.

(Note: the fact that profit can be represented in a single number does not mean that a business is a single-indicator system. Profit is a unique metric in that it is a combination of lots of different metrics as well as every decision made within an organization. Thus, it encapsulates both a synchronic and a diachronic perspective.)

If we wanted, we could (and businesses often do this) break that larger metric into its component parts in an attempt to see patterns and search for causal clues and the reasons behind the overall numbers. In addition, while profit is always the goal, no quarterly or annual report of a business' profit is complete without an extensive description of how those profits were achieved and the plans the organization has for future success. (That is far different than the synchronic measure discussed in the last chapter.)

Any number that can communicate such a significant amount of information that simply and cleanly will not be a passive observer within an accountability package but a very active participant. By that I mean that the idea represented in the metric will always skew the regular activity of the business in its direction. That can be a major skew, such as when a CEO invests in a new product line or makes the decision to purchase a competitor as a means toward future profits, or a minor one, where someone in a purchasing office chooses to buy pencils from the vendor who is a few cents cheaper than its competition.

Regardless, whatever happens in a company contributes to the organization's ability to turn a profit, and those who don't find themselves supporting that sort of skew are likely to be shown the door.

We could say, then, that a proper accountability package in corporate America has two components to it: the formal and informal programs that an employee uses to gauge and guide their behavior, and the metric of profit, all of which combine to create that culture I spoke of.

Education reformers for as long as we have had education reform believed that schools, too, should adopt an accountability package that could create an optimal culture. And I agree: the educational disparities between various socioeconomic groups have long been something that is entirely unacceptable, all kids really do deserve a shot at a high-quality education, and teachers who aren't interested in being active participants in that process should go do something else for a living.

Everyone inside and outside of education should see an accountability package capable of creating and fomenting that type of culture as a good thing.

Instead, policymakers committed an act of synecdoche and positioned reading and math scores as the proxy for everything that happens in schools, suggesting that all of the accountabilities regarding schooling can be wrapped up in two numbers.

The question we now must ask ourselves is this: Will the result be akin to a company that focuses on revenue and doesn't concern itself with actual profit, or a carpenter who can only make table legs? Or do reading and mathematics test scores really encapsulate everything that happens in a school such that they aren't two parts standing in for a much larger whole but are instead reflective of the whole?

Answering that question is actually easy, and it has nothing to do with how important reading and math are as subjects.

First, let's just accept as a given that the vast majority of schools and school districts in this country have some sort of annual formal evaluation in place, and that, of course, they all have the informal component. In some cases the formal component is extensive, holding new teachers to strict requirements during a mentoring phase while they learn the ropes and then providing formal feedback to everyone throughout the year, and in others it's a perfunctory ritual little more than a rubber stamp.

My point here is not to criticize any of the choices a school leader makes regarding how best to carry out the formal and informal components of the accountability package but to point out that they exist and to some degree always have.

This means that the early complaints regarding our school's inability to meet our expectations can be interpreted to some degree as a complaint about how these two components were being managed.

Perhaps the culture in the school inadvertently tolerated low expectations for the students given the impoverished nature of its surroundings. Perhaps the formal evaluation system was so out of touch with reality that it couldn't motivate or at some point dismiss the anecdotal teacher we have all at some point read about, who simply read the paper during first period every day as if daring anyone to fire him.

My own opinion is that both were lacking. I could point out that principals are given almost no management training, and that unlike people in industry who spend a good part of each day watching their supervisors manage and learning from that process, teachers—just prior to becoming principals and assistant principals—spend most of their time instructing students.

Or I could point out that of the six major organizations that I have worked for every single one of them had systems that were imperfect and could stand to be improved, and that most certainly is also the case for schools. My brother and I often joke that every company has problems: you just have to pick the problems you think you can deal with and join that company. That isn't a criticism of any company, but an acknowledgment that companies (and schools) are made of people and people are imperfect.

Regardless of the reason, reformers were right to point out that the formal and informal components of the package were in need of improvement, and in that sense I think they deserve a great deal of credit. Mountains of literature now exist offering ways to do that, and school leadership as an issue now receives far more attention than it did in the past. That has to be seen as a good thing.

Regarding the third piece of the industry-based accountability package, reformers were all too aware that they lacked any sort of unifying metric.

Those responsible for funding and patrolling education have made any number of attempts to impose just such a metric. A simple prereform attempt occurred in the late 1960s and carried on through to the advent of school reform. Schools that received certain forms of federal funding were required to report standardized test scores for students impacted by that funding.

Another attempt occurred in the 1980s and 1990s. Under the recognition that the test scores provided only a partial lens into what schools were doing, states started creating school report cards to document levels of spending and a variety of achievement indicators such as the number of Advanced Placement tests passed, the hours of professional development taken by teachers, and of course test results.

These certainly gave a more complete picture of a school, but they were tough to interpret. It is one thing, for example, to see that your school is in the twenty-fifth percentile regarding per student funding, the fiftieth percentile in terms of mathematics test scores, and the fifteenth percentile in terms of AP classes passed. It is quite another to know what to do with that information, and it still didn't distill into a single metric.

The loudest criticism of most of these attempts, however, was that other than the standardized test scores most of the rest of the data being reported had to do with inputs and not outputs. What concerned those funding and patrolling education was that the outcomes seemed inadequate considering the investment.

Indeed, numerous studies provided compelling evidence that certain segments of the population were being woefully underserved in spite of the investment, which was more than enough to justify the concern. The response under the Clinton administration was that states were required for the first time to produce output test scores for *all* of their students in certain grades in key subject areas and to show improvement under them, and then under the second Bush's first administration the requirement was put on steroids when No Child Left Behind (NCLB) was passed and extended to additional grades and the penalties for noncompliance were greatly expanded.

Both represented gestures that suffered from policymakers not understanding what a test was or the circumstances in which they were designed to work, and in both cases the policies far exceeded the designs of the tests chosen to carry that weight.

NCLB required that virtually every student in grades three through eight and in grade ten participate in standardized tests in reading and mathematics during each year of their schooling, and that these tests are to serve as the primary quality determination for schools. The law's key requirement was this: by some future date (it changed several times), 100 percent of all schools need to ensure that 100 percent of all students answer a sufficient number of items on a standardized test correctly or the school will be declared a failure and possibly taken over or reconstituted.

Those items need to come from state-developed content standards, and those standards need to serve as the basis for the curriculum.

Forgetting for a moment that test scores have nothing to say about educational quality but merely show the distribution of schools and students at a particular moment in time (see the chapter on testing), where we now seem to find ourselves is with an accountability package in education that is supposed to mirror the package in industry and drive education forward in a positive direction. That parallelism was completed—so it seems—with reading and mathematics test scores being assigned the same rhetorical function as "profit" in the business world.

Profitability and a test score, however, are not even in the same semantic ballpark. The amount of profit a company earns is a composite of every single decision that happens within that company throughout the course of a year.

A janitor sweeping the floors earns a wage for doing that work and impacts the amount of profit that is earned. Sales people winning or losing sales do as well. Decisions as to whether or not to invest in new products or product lines, which pencils to buy, how much to charge customers, and what the advertising budget will be all go to the bottom line as reflected by how profitable the company winds up being at the end of the year. Profit is not a *proxy*—it is the very measure itself.

A standardized test score is a proxy that estimates where a student or a school fit when compared to others as of a single point in time. A test score doesn't even pretend to represent everything that happens during the times in the classrooms where reading and mathematics are taught, and it cannot even begin to offer comment on what happens regarding the other two-thirds of what occurs in schools.

In fact, if you'll recall, a standardized test score does its job only if the tested content isn't anticipated, and that job is to provide a comparative point of view of a single point in time, only that is no way a *summary* of anything that occurred.

Test scores being assigned the same rhetorical role in the school accountability package as profitability in the industry package has some far-reaching consequences.

First, as does the idea of profits, the idea of a test score as a metric of success skews the system. At the surface level the effect of the skew is easy to see: more hours devoted to reading and mathematics and fewer to subjects such as art, music, dance, and drama.[1] The skew, though, goes well beyond the selection of courses, going into the classroom where it urges an additional skew toward higher scores on standardized tests.

This should not be a surprise. If a test score in education is supposed to be parallel to the profit motive in a business, the surprise would be if such a skew didn't exist. The whole point and value in having such a metric is to insist on that sort of skew—which, by the way, is why some organizations function explicitly as nonprofits: they find the skew toward profits to be out of sync with their primary purpose for existence (perhaps there is a lesson to be learned here).

The skew in schools toward higher standardized test scores, however, is not toward the notion of educational quality. A standardized test exists, by design, to offer a point of comparison for schools and students. The resulting test scores are then completely silent as to their cause. Even when used as designed, they cannot comment on the quality of the school that produced them because they have not been imbued with any capacity to do so.

Just because one school is higher or lower on the distribution than another on its own is meaningless. It has no notion of what decisions produced it or whether those were good or bad decisions, and it cannot therefore comment on its own about the appropriateness of any decision yet to be made.

It may be that the school with the lower scores is in a poor neighborhood but that it is successful year in and year out keeping dropouts to a minimum, curbing the school violence that plagues its neighbors, and graduating students at an impressive rate, and that the school with higher test scores is in a rich suburb and will get those kind of results with hardly any effort at all. Remember, a standardized test score has no capacity to make a quality judgment regarding any school.

However, a skew toward a higher test score may allow a great many who falsely equate such a thing with educational quality to believe they have steered the educational enterprise in the right direction, but the nature of what a standardized test is belies that.

Second, assigning the same rhetorical role to test scores as to profit means that policymakers accept as a point of fact the notion that success against the metric is always a good thing. When a company is profitable (within, of course, the laws that govern such a thing), shareholders, owners, and the management of the companies can feel that they have done their job.

Since test scores now operate as a similar metric to profits, that same assumption applies: that a high or rising test score is always a good thing. But is it? We showed in the last chapter that not only is a test score silent as to its cause but also that it can be made to rise for all the wrong reasons: it can be *manipulated.*

A school can move test scores higher from one year to the next with a teach-to-the-test mentality, and they may be able to maintain them at those levels over time once the curriculum is sufficiently aligned with the test, all while failing to actually provide a quality education for their students.

Profits—earned within the rules—mean that the leaders of a company are doing what they were hired to do because the profit metric represents a distillation of all the decisions within the company—both good and bad—and their combined effect on the condition of the business.

Test scores do nothing of the sort. They are in no way a summary of everything that happened in a school or a classroom, and as a proxy and a point-in-time estimate they lack any of the meanings behind the calculation of profits. Even when used properly, test scores were not designed (I'm a bit of a broken record here) to say anything about educational quality.

Assuming that test scores should motivate in the same way as profits may be a semantically pleasing thing to say, but the fact is that they cannot—it isn't in their nature.

Third, assigning test scores the same role as profits in an educational accountability package forgets the fact that unlike a test score the profitability metric in no way limits the infinite variety of ways it can be met, and in fact it encourages new ways to make it happen.

Limits are a function of the industry in which you work as well as your job, and it is up to each to determine how best within the limits of their position to make that contribution: consultants focus on the quality of their advice; buyers for a manufacturing company focus on the quality and constancy of raw materials and sourced parts; the supervisor on an assembly line works hard to ensure a consistent outcome; and a project manager for a government contractor focuses on his or her ability to manage large, complex programs and bring them in on time and on budget.

The accountability metric of reading and mathematics test scores, however, is unapologetically limiting regarding a host of behaviors. Consider the nature of the NCLB requirement in its most pragmatic sense: all students in a school will earn a particular score on a standardized test in order for the school to be considered as doing its job. In that sense the metric insists upon an approach wherein all teachers teaching in grades three through eight and

grade ten behave such that all their students perform similarly on the tests on about the same day each year.

The requirement infers that full success at the system level will occur once teachers can receive a batch of students who all performed similarly on a standardized test the year before, who will then march through a year's worth of carefully controlled instruction, and then be able to perform similar to each other once again on a different version of the standardized test.

The contradictions within such a vision—and to the selected processes for measuring it—are numerous:

First, a classroom of kids is by definition a deeply heterogeneous group, and as of any moment in time it will differ in terms of their needs, their social and emotional states, their learning and coping strategies, and whatever happened yesterday. Any strategy based on the assumption that you can homogenize such a group or the instruction they are to receive is likely to fail. That simply runs counter to what and who people are.

Second, the selected measure of a standardized test is valid only when it can show the distribution of students, and yet the requirement against it is for all students to perform similarly. As has been discussed, when all students perform similarly on an item the item is now useless for the purpose of a standardized test, and new items that will help discriminate the differences among students will need to be selected. A requirement that all students perform similarly on a test designed to identify distributions is just silly and makes no sense.

The third contradiction is the one that actually concerns me the most. A classroom is supposed to be a dynamic place of learning in which trained professionals search out the best means by which to deliver a quality education to each student. But the policy's vision of a successful system is one of students entering a classroom in a predictable fashion, learning in a predictable fashion, and then performing on a test in a predictable fashion.

That sounds to me much more like what happens in a manufacturing firm, in which raw product that meets certain specifications is put through a set of processes that produce a finished product that meets a new set of specifications. That is the wrong metaphor through which to view the education of a child, a complete contradiction to what a teacher's role is, and it demeans the profession, even when the effects of it are just felt and aren't articulated as bluntly as I have laid them out here.

The bottom line is that we may want a metric in education similar to profitability in business, but reading and mathematics scores from standardized tests are incapable of offering themselves as such a metric without doing serious damage to the larger system.

One other point is critical here regarding this notion that the accountability model in business based on the metric of profits should be brought to bear on schools. One of the largest differences between schools and a business is in the fundamental role of leadership. In a business, leadership is ultimately about ensuring the survival of the company, but in a school, leadership is ultimately about the survival of those the organization serves.

This translates to decisions being made in very different ways. The bottom line is that a CEO has the fiduciary responsibility to put the company first and to ensure that it is sufficiently fit so that it can turn a profit now and well into the future. He/she cannot do that without customers, but the customers are a means to an internal end.

For an educator, the responsibility is to the student, who is external to the actual structure of a school, and the school provides the means by which to fulfill that responsibility. Asking an educational leader to adopt a more corporate approach to accountability risks asking an educator to put the survival of the school ahead of what might be good for the student and treat the students as a means to an end.

Consider the choice that a school leader is faced with under the current weight of our school accountability systems: do I deploy a rich curriculum that will serve students well for the long term, or do I resort to a teach-to-the-test mentality for fear that students will do poorly on the test and then I may lose my job, along with my fellow teachers, many of whom don't even teach reading or math?

Teachers are not consultants competing with one another to sell their services, nor are they manufacturers of wisdom as a salable item. Children and their parents aren't customers choosing one product or service over another. Instead, a teacher spends all day attempting to impact a student's learning in a manner helpful to the student, while a CEO spends all day attempting to impact a consumer's behavior to make a choice that is advantageous to the company.

A teacher spends his or her time managing student learning with the school as the vehicle that makes that possible. A CEO spends his or her time managing a company toward a profit, and the customers in turn make that possible.

Before I go on to the final section of this chapter, I want to return for a moment to a notion discussed in the beginning chapter regarding the idea that you can attempt to convince the world that something is broken as a means to changing it, or you can work from the position that anything can be improved and attempt to offer those improvements, with an argument as to the benefits the improvement offers.

The value of the latter is that you don't need to convince anyone that anything is necessarily wrong, because if you can make the argument for an improvement compelling enough by setting forth a vision for what can be, that can often be enough.

The reform movement chose the path of declaring education broken and has now spent the last thirty years offering up its repairs, with a very mixed set of results that are in no way commensurate with the effort or the investment.

I argued then and I repeat it now that the preferred approach would have been the one that put us on a path of improvement, and I want to be clear that while I am deeply critical of many of the choices that have been made, I would save my harshest criticism for the manner in which they have been made. Working from a position that everything is broken allows the policy community to haphazardly pick and choose what to impose using the rationale that anything has to be better than what we had.

That is perhaps the most critical lesson we could learn from the business community that has all but been ignored, in that a business is a large, complex system, and in order to make good decisions it requires a deep understanding of those systems so that decisions can be made with the entire system in mind. Only then are the decisions actually beneficial to the organization.

We are going to have to be critical—very critical—regarding the path by which we arrived at this point, particularly because we have to understand what has happened in order to not let it happen again. But moving forward I would hope we take the improvement track—I don't think education can survive another thirty years of operating under a reform-style paradigm.

To say it ever more bluntly, I fear that reform as an idea may be fundamentally "broken," but I refuse to work from that formal position since I think it would be an act of lunacy to repeat what we have done over the past thirty years under the banner of a new name.

What should be clear by this point regarding the quality determination in schools is that a very small indicator from within a very large system is now used to judge the entire system even though by design the test scores selected for the job have nothing to say regarding educational quality.

That is a pickle, by any stretch of the imagination.

Education is going to have to find a set of metrics that can function much more along the lines of profit. I believe this because absent such metrics policymakers will likely continue down the testing road under the erroneous assumption that something is better than nothing. Educators need to be far more pragmatic than that. We must criticize, absolutely, but we must offer a set of alternatives if a better system really is the goal.

Consider what the criteria for such metrics would need to be, given that such metrics will skew the behaviors within schools in their direction:

1. Every employee within a school needs to see himself or herself within the metric so that they can skew their own behaviors in the direction of the metric.
2. The metrics need to relate to behaviors that are within people's control so that no one feels helpless against them.
3. The metrics need to have immediate credibility with a wider audience.
4. The metrics need to produce a result that can be meaningfully compared to others.
5. The metrics need to be designed such that each can produce a judgment related to educational quality.

In order to replicate what the profit metric does for business, it will take multiple metrics in education. Educating children is a far more complex affair than achieving a profit goal, and that complexity warrants a metrics system that respects that fact. Policymakers need to accept that in this case simple is not better.

Here are four ideas for metrics that fit these criteria that would create situations in which serving the needs of the organization and serving the needs of the student are one and the same, and that fit the criteria above. These are just ideas, and even then they offer just a smattering for what is possible, but they should provide a sense of the flavor of metrics that meet the criteria:

- Percentage of those who enter college, the military, or are gainfully employed one year following graduation. Calculating the metric would require calculating the size of the cohort when it entered high school and dividing it by the number of students enrolled in college, who joined the military, or who are gainfully employed six months following graduation. The easiest way to skew in the direction of the metric is to increase the number of students working (military is work, of course) or attending school, as the metric will quickly improve as that happens. That also means encouraging students to stay in school and do well, since the studies are clear regarding the increased opportunities that come with each additional year of high school study. Achieving such a skew could be a part of every school employee's evaluation, since everyone would have some sort of contribution to make, even if it was just attitudinal. Little value would come in a single measure, but the comparisons over time would be deeply meaningful.
- For elementary and middle schools, the total number of instructional hours lost to absenteeism, by classroom, grade, and school. When makeup work is performed, half of lost hours represented in the work would be credited back to the school. The skew here is twofold: work hard on all fronts to ensure that the students make it to class, and then work hard to address the

makeup work so the negative impact on the metric is minimized. Over time, it would be entirely possible to determine whether or not the rate was improving and to determine what activities led to the least number of instructional hours being missed. Improvement over time on the metric could be a part of the principal's and every teacher's annual evaluation in a fair and unbiased manner.

- For all schools, the percentages of students in the school who report in an annual survey how frequently teachers call them by their names. The research is clear that students who have a sense of belonging will fare better in school, and one of the clearest indicators for this is whether a student believes the teachers know they exist.[2] The skew is again clear: know the students' names and use them. A principal could easily lead this effort with a photo of each student on the wall of the teacher's lounge, impromptu contests for faculty who can name the most students, and an indicator on each teacher's annual evaluation regarding how the school fared on the metric.

- For each school the percentage of students enrolled in the school who have met each of the established standards—but *fulfillment standards*: write well once each year; as part of a high school requirement perform a play, write a short novel, or perform an original song; and more, as well as the percentage of students who accomplished the standard within its assigned year. The school-based approach would serve as an academic indicator for the school by showing how well it served its students prior to matriculation to a new school, and the grade-based approach would ensure that every effort was made by staff to see that a student could meet each standard during an assigned year, but if that was not possible that it was met during the student's stay at the school.

The reason I would argue that these four metrics are powerful is because, like the profit metric, every part of the organization can get behind them and offer support. They aren't at risk of offering a "part for the whole" approach, but rather, they become indicators, like profit, of how a school is actually performing.

Each of these possible metrics and a host of other candidates will skew the behaviors of each school employee and hold them accountable for doing so, but that behavior is also good for the students.

And not every metric would be necessary or even helpful in every school. I can think of some high-performing suburban high schools that would perform very well regarding the first metric in spite of what actually happens in the schools, so the overall metric may not be very meaningful for them. However, research shows that in these same schools that students who transfer in as well as their minority students do not fare nearly so well. The standard for such a school, then, may focus on those students in particular and on improving the metric for those students over time.

School is simply too multifaceted a place to reduce the activity to a single metric, or some form of a single metric. We do far more harm than good when we attempt to do so.

The fact that reading and mathematics standardized tests are not included as accountability metrics in the suggestions above—for all the reasons that have been and will continue to be discussed—doesn't mean that a metric that doesn't include them is soft or doesn't care about academics.

A rich set of metrics that included all sorts of fulfillment standards will require teachers with a deep content knowledge and understanding of their fields to impart a great deal of that to students in the process of working to meet them, and compliance with those standards is impossible absent that understanding.

The best way to ensure that a student will be gainfully employed or in school one year after graduation is to provide them the requisite skills to ensure that they have what it takes to experience that success.

The best way to ensure that every teacher has the opportunity to teach and every student to learn is to get them together in a classroom, and when for reasons beyond anyone's control that doesn't happen, to get the student caught up as quickly as possible.

And the best means to ensure that students are able to meet a robust fulfillment standard is to work with them as they attempt to meet the standard so that they learn well the material they need in the process.

Metrics that can drive the sorts of behaviors that are good for students, schools, and the educators in them are critical. None of them is measurable via a standardized test.

NOTES

1. Basmat Parsad and Maura Spiegleman, *Arts Education in Elementary and Secondary Schools, 1999–2000 and 2009–2010* (Washington, DC: The National Center for Educational Statistics, Institute of Education Sciences, U.S. Department of Education, 2012), 12, 22, 29, 35, 44, 50.

2. Russ Quaglia, "Student Aspirations: A Critical Dimension in Effective Schools," *Research in Rural Education* 6, no. 2 (1989): 7.

Chapter Eight

Locating Success

Let's say you've made it this far in my argument and that you aren't convinced about anything that I've said, that you still truly believe that the standards as they exist are just fine, and that success against the tested content is just a matter of everyone trying harder.

Let's bracket that as a given and test it. Rather than critique the accountability system we have for a few minutes, let's assume that we have all the tools we need in order to define and motivate student success. Let's examine what a truly successful system would look like *within* the constraints of the *current* system so that we can see what qualifies as success and if that success is in fact in line with our expectations.

When we bracket the argument in that way, of course, we have to assume that the form educational standards take is acceptable—far better than nothing—and that somewhere in them is the level of success we expect for our students. We have to also assume that we made a good choice selecting standardized tests as the vehicle for the quality determination, and that those who argue otherwise are a bunch of stuffy academics who like to sit around in an ivory tower and throw stones.

I'm going to focus the discussion on the point in which success in a school is determined, since it is the key component in the current evaluation system of a school, far outweighing all the other elements. If the system as it stands has the chance to be successful, it has to have properly located the success determination. Everything else hinges on that point.

If the constraints in the current system still allow for all students to be successful against the broader goals of education reform, then I would have to rethink my argument because I will have shown that the issue is in fact one of *implementation*. If it does not, then it should strengthen the argument I have presented so far.

I'm going to address five "features" of the current system that all have to do with how we define success in schools to see if any of those features in fact leads us to a definition of success in line with our expectations for schools. That seems the simplest and most direct route I can think of for understanding if "success" in the current system equates to what most believe "success" in schools should look like. The features are as follows:

1. The "line in the sand" drawn at a particular test score that serves as the point defining success. Sometimes this is referred to as a passing score, and other times as "meeting" the standard, "proficient," or some similar term.
2. More "rigorous" tests, which is when education reformers ask for tougher tests as the means to advance the system toward excellence.
3. Adaptive testing, which is a form of standardized testing that can offer more precise estimates of achievement for every student.
4. Value-added models, which are accountability models that attempt to measure how far students have advanced from one year to the next and then ask teachers to be accountable for the amount of growth over time.
5. Equity, in which the idea is to have the same standard for all children so that we can be said to realize that the goal of education is the same no matter the circumstances under which a child was born or is being educated.

The point in selecting these five is that my argument risks being invalid if any of these stands a chance of defining success in a manner commensurate with the broader goals of education. Thus they are worthy subjects for exploration in this light.

FEATURE #1: DRAWING A LINE IN THE SAND

At some point in the not-so-distant past someone drew a line in the sand just above a particular score on an educational test and labeled it "meeting" the standard or "proficient" against the standard, and now everyone is doing it. You've no doubt heard these type of scores reported in the local newspapers or seen them on your children's reports. That line defines success for the student and the school. The assumption is that such a score means that the school has done its job, and the student has as well. That line defines success.

This seemingly helpful gesture of assigning labels to educational test scores is a staple in high-stakes tests, such as those taken by prospective doctors, nurses, and engineers to prove to the world that their training has properly prepared them to treat us when we are sick and build buildings that won't fall down in a storm.

They offer protection for society against those who lack the actual knowledge and skills to perform the tasks that will be required of them, and an assurance to the field that the candidate is ready to enter professional life. A nursing, medical, or engineering student who passes such exams can be said to have accomplished something significant.

Setting that sort of cut score is no simple task. The content needs to be evaluated such that professionals already in the field can make an estimation of how much of the content that makes up the field needs to have been mastered in order to admit the hopeful professionals into the field.

This is a painstaking process that generally involves one of two approaches: in the first approach, evaluators make estimates regarding the percentage of minimally competent test takers they believe would answer each item correctly, in effect identifying the significance of each item. In the second approach, the test items are lined up from the easiest item to the most difficult item in terms of the percentage of respondents that answered each correctly, and evaluators draw a line at the point that they believe represents the measure of success.

Either of those methodologies can then have all the evaluations combined to form the single point that defines success or failure. (Again, an apology to the measurement community as this is an oversimplification, but it gets the point across.)

In the end, the cut score defines the point at which doctors, nurses, and engineers are made. One point above it means you could begin your career, and one point below it means you have to wait and try again another day. The point is always at risk of being a bit arbitrary, since the fact of the matter is that virtually no difference exists between a student, that scores one point above and another that scores one point below the cut score. Nevertheless, those two scores are interpreted very differently: one student is declared worthy of entering the profession, while one is not.

The arbitrariness aside, it should be obvious why the cut scores from professional exams were seen as a value-add to standardized tests in education: doctors, nurses, and engineers who passed very difficult tests were deemed worthy to enter their professions, and education at the time was looking around for any means possible to shore up what was perceived to be a shaky enterprise at best.

To add the panache of a professional licensure exam stood to be a good step.

But educational tests are very different from a certification or licensure exam. A licensure exam is built so that it will show a distribution across all of the candidates *who want to gain entrance to a field* and is designed to allow that to happen only for *some* of those candidates.

Examinees *self-select* their way into the exam and are thus *motivated* to do their best because the rewards are huge. The items and the exams that are comprised of them are intentionally quite difficult, even for people who managed to spend years preparing for that very moment. To even take a licensure exam, examinees have to prove themselves worthy by taking the requisite number of courses, and examinees take the test at a point in time *when examinees deem themselves to be ready.*

Many of the items on licensure exams are such that all of the options given are correct, but given the details in the item concerning symptoms, the conditions of the patient, or the challenge of the structural problem in a building, one is more right than the others. You had better have directly learned that sort of material or you have a very small chance of answering such an item correctly.

You are being admitted to a field of professionals if you pass, and that field needs to see you as credible.

A standardized test in education is built so that leaders and researchers can compare one school group to another, which requires content that about half the targeted population of students will answer correctly. The reward structure for educational tests is also very different—students may attempt to do well to avoid being labeled as a failure, but success on such tests has little bearing on the student's long-term success. It is not a matter of life or death for students to perform well on such tests, so the motivation factor is almost opposite that of a certification exam. One is seen as a perfunctory chore with the potential for mostly potential negative consequences for failure, while the other is a gateway to a career.

The content on educational exams remains curriculum neutral (in the sense that teaching to the test will invalidate the results), and the test is administered on a date certain each year on a ready-or-not basis. No student or teacher has a say in whether the student is ready to tackle the content—it isn't that type of content. The content wasn't selected because it is the most pertinent within a domain but because it does the job of showing the distribution of students within that domain.

You can draw and label lines in the sand for these two very different types of tests, but although the labels may be similar the underlying meanings are not. While both tests require examinees to answer a sufficient number of items in order to pass, the nature of those items—driven by the different purposes of the tests—differs a great deal.

Drawing a line in the sand on a test that by definition does not contain anywhere within it the material most relevant to the domain does not mean that somehow the correct answers can magically combine to be more than the sum of their parts and directly reference the domain.

At best, the cut score might serve as a proxy for the larger domain—though this is a stretch—but only if no one anticipated the test in the curriculum. If the content to be tested was anticipated in any way, then the cut score isn't a proxy at all, but a direct measure of the degree to which the test became the curriculum and children were damaged in the process.

The line in the sand on a test designed for limited use within a school and a line in the sand designed to keep those who aren't yet qualified out of a profession do not by any stretch of the imagination mean the same thing. We may want them to, but that would be impossible.

One other point from the testing chapter is important here. The point of a standardized test is to identify the differences in a population of students and show that in a distribution. A test that fails to do that fails as a test.

That point runs counter to the idea in a cut score that we want all students to achieve at or above that level on such tests. In fact, the idea that all students would do well on such a test is a bit of an oxymoron. It can certainly happen in individual schools just like it does for individual students, but when it happens across the entire test the test designer has made a mistake. If you set a cut score on such a test and insist that all students cross that threshold you are asking the test to work against type—you are asking it to work beyond its design.

Licensure exams don't have this problem. The cut score on these exams is *intended* to prevent lots of people from passing. A test that shows the distribution of candidates allows you to reject the candidates who score below a certain point, so the cut score never risks asking the test takers to work against the design of the test.

So—where is success according to the labels we apply to cut scores on educational tests? It is in the test itself, a test of limited content, and even then, perhaps only the portion of the content below the passing score. But try though we might, moving all students past any established cut score is antithetical to the design of such tests. Not everyone can or will pass their medical boards—that is explicit in the design. Not everyone will achieve a relatively high score on a standardized educational assessment. That, too, is explicit in its design.

Nevertheless, the entire accountability system is built around the assumption that a cut score on a standardized test means a great deal more than it ever can. That assumption includes the quality determination for the student and their entire year, the teacher and their entire year, and the school and every decision made within it during the year.

I said in an earlier chapter that the dominant form underlying our present educational standards is a behavioral standard that describes what a student should do regarding educational behavior but does not answer questions as to how good is good enough. Advocates of establishing cut scores on tests (I know because I was once one of them) realized that the squishiness in behavioral educational standards meant that the "good enough" question would need to be answered elsewhere and proposed end-of-year tests as the basis for making that determination.

The real standards, then, the ones we care about the most, aren't in our written standards, and certainly aren't in the tests we ask students to take each year, leaving us with a very important question: Where are they?

And since we don't know or they don't seem to be where we expected them to be, we need to be very careful that we don't promote a system that can never live up to its promise. We need to be very wary when we hear that someone has "met" the standard on one of the annual accountability tests that are part of the current accountability systems, because the "success" that it represents isn't quite what it purports to be.

FEATURE #2: MORE "RIGOROUS" TESTS

For those who accept that the current system is fine but that it just needs some tweaking, this call for "more rigorous tests" is a pretty common one. You hear such a call from any number of beltway organizations, reformers, governors, and mayors on any given day of any given week.

I've had my say regarding the sloppy semantics in using the work *rigor* as an adjective that is assumed to reference the idea that education should offer up a greater challenge to students, but let's just accept—since that is what this chapter is doing—that more challenging ("rigorous") tests and higher (also "rigorous") passing scores would be a step in the right direction.

The idea behind the choice for standardized testing seemed to be a "rising tide lifts all boats" approach. It is certainly true that if we change the status quo for the better in education (and don't teach to the test) that the types of test items that half of students would miss would change: they would become more difficult than those that went before.

Seeing that change is tricky, since the items always have to "behave" in their predictable manner in order to work, and it is difficult to see a change over time between two items that half of the students missed. Test professionals accomplish that task by nailing down a point when a testing program begins so that changes relative to that original point can be noted.

Nailing down this original point allows test designers to change out test items from one year to the next and still have the scores mean the same things. To do this, test designers select some arbitrary scale, like 200–900 or some such thing, for use in reporting results. Each year the differences between tests are ironed out in a very technical process called equating, but rather than create a confusing chart that shows this year's scores all being two points easier than last year's but a point harder than the year before, all the scores are converted to the same scale to aid with interpretation.

That way scores from one year to the next can be easily and quickly compared in spite of the fact that the test items may change and the overall test may therefore be a little harder or a little easier than the one the year before.

In theory, it would be possible that over a period of years each cohort of students passing through a grade would be much smarter than the cohort before it. As the test items were changed out over that period, it would require progressively more difficult items in order for them to behave in a predictable manner (the fifty-fifty rule again), since that particular grade of students was getting smarter with each passing year.

Should that happen, the number of items answered correctly by students wouldn't likely change very much, but the scale score would climb dramatically. It is even conceivable in my hypothetical model to imagine a future point where the highest-performing students from year one and the lowest-performing students from a future year actually score similarly, so great has been the improvement.

That really is a compelling (hypothetical) vision when you think about it: a test designed as an approximation for the status quo is then capable of capturing the changes in that status quo over time, providing evidence that something great has happened.

If that could be shown to be true, it would mean that the test (hypothetically) isn't the limiting factor to greatness at all, but rather, that dubious distinction is somewhere else. I'm not saying this tongue-in-cheek either, and I'm not going to argue against this point later. Standardized tests properly used in the background are designed to show just this sort of change should it occur, and if the change is that dramatic the design of such tests will allow them to record it in a believable manner.

The call for more rigorous tests seems to indicate a desire for just this sort of thing to happen, for the future's low performers to be where our high performers are today. But the call seems to be one that wants us to hurry the process along, to get the harder tests out ahead of the tested populations' ability to handle the material as a means to jump-starting things.

If the test is to jump-start the movement toward greatness, then the assumption is that we should include items ahead of the point in time when they might actually behave appropriately to be included on a standardized test.

We would, in that situation, include some additional items that 80, 90, or even 100 percent of students would answer incorrectly, since we were attempting to increase the difficulty level of the test, setting a higher bar for students and schools to jump over. Because of the scaling and equating process from one year to the next, we could still report the differences in achievement from one year to the next, even though lots of students missed lots of those very difficult items.

We could do that because we could still compare students back to that original point we nailed down from the initial administration, which would allow us to compare the performance from our much more difficult test with those that came before.

We need to be honest about the impact of these very difficult items that have been added to the test on the final scaled test score, because the truth is that until they start behaving in a predictable manner, it won't be much. The impact of a very easy or a very difficult item is actually washed out during the scaling and equating processes.

Such items will contribute to making the overall test easier or more difficult than the previous year's tests, and those differences need to be ironed out so that the scores from both years can be compared. Scores at the extreme ends stand very little chance of making any distributive contribution, and so from a technical perspective they don't much matter. That's why in the tests I took when I was in school those items were excluded. They added to the length and cost of the test and yet added no information regarding how I stacked up against my peers.

That means that there remains only one way that the more difficult items can have any impact at all, and it isn't because the curriculum got more challenging—if that had happened and proved successful then the items would have become more difficult naturally, since it would require a more difficult item to meet the fifty-fifty threshold. The only way that our new, more difficult items can have an immediate impact is if *they serve as the basis for teaching*—sanctioning the idea that teaching to the test is a perfectly acceptable thing to do.

Of course, if someone chooses to teach to the test that immediately invalidates the results, and what is left are all the consequences for having done so discussed so far. I refer you back to the chapter on testing as a refresher on why teaching to a standardized test is never an acceptable thing to do, why it invalidates a test score, and how it damages the long-term chances for a student.

A test designed as a statistical representation of the status quo—whether that be today or one we hope to have in the future—cannot also serve as the lever by which you move that status quo.

Such tests are designed for passive observers only and not active participants in the process. As soon as you make them an active participant, you position success inside them, even when—in fact, especially when—you attempt to make them "more rigorous."

The fallacy here is that making tests harder offers the policy community a chance to increase the quality of education. That runs completely counter to what a standardized test is and the conditions under which it is designed to work.

The second call for "more rigorous tests" involves raising the passing score on the existing exams. It should come as no surprise that an examination of the content below the passing score on state tests looks astonishingly simple in most cases, and that a common response would be that of course students should be able to answer at least the majority of those items. That is inherent in the design.

Those who focus on the content have no problem suggesting that a higher passing score is warranted, and they have very little problem getting others to go along. I have seen any number of very impressive presentations that show released test items that are easier than the item just below the passing score accompanied by the somewhat stunned reaction that only about half of the students who took the exam answered them correctly.

But then, that is precisely why that particular item was selected for inclusion and not some other similar item that all the students answered correctly. Something about the item the presenter showed on the screen helped to identify the distribution of students because about half of the students answered it incorrectly.

That isn't due to a flaw in the students but because of how the item was intended to function. Putting up such items and declaring that they represent a low bar misses that very critical point.

What is obvious in the call for increasing the passing scores is the same desire that exists in the call for more difficult tests for the "rising tide" effect to lift the system over time. In my hypothetical example in which I eventually had the lowest-performing students of the future scoring similar to today's highest-performing students, the idea regarding a passing score would be to nudge the passing score up until it matched someone's definition of being high enough and then lock it into place.

In the years that follow, the rising tide should one day ensure that all students perform at or above that level. That notion, by the way, is exactly what the No Child Left Behind legislation attempted to put into place.

If we accept the premise that just such a vision is possible, that a system that simultaneously raises the difficulty level of the test and the passing score can result in real greatness, we must also accept that once again we are asking the test to get out ahead of the students and do what it was not designed to do.

The first time a passing score was added to an accountability test served to define what success looked like for the student, the school, and the teacher. That was not a subtle message—teachers and school administrations were told they would be replaced if they failed to move their students across that hurdle. Now that the original passing scores are being perceived as being too low, the next gesture will be to move that score up, placing a few more items beneath it, but the fact that this is being proposed as an incentive to move the system means that they expect teachers to pay attention to the test as the primary advisor for what should be included in the curriculum!

The original gesture of accountability to a cut score suggested that teachers look, and behind the idea of raising it is an insistence that teachers do just that.

Consider, however, that the focal point of a passing score is considerably lower than the most difficult items on a test. The material right up to the passing score is the material that if taught will give teachers the most bang for the buck—it is the material that most of their students stand the greatest chance of getting right.

The material above the passing score offers a somewhat lower rate of return, since no matter how hard they work fewer students will answer those items correctly, and to be honest, students need not answer those items in order to pass and be declared successful. That is how the test was designed to work!

I am not, of course, suggesting that teachers have access to the test ahead of time (although states almost always release some items each year, and some states release the entire test), but teachers are as intuitive as anyone else and know that the most difficult material on the test isn't required for students to pass. Each and every student could miss the most difficult pieces of the content and 100 percent of them could still perform just slightly above the cut score.

A teacher faced with a challenging population is going to spend time as efficiently as possible in helping his or her students achieve success. As the bar is moved up, the new definition of success is the old plus a few more items, but it still risks excluding the most relevant material, either because it is above the cut score or it isn't on the test to begin with.

In short, the idea of moving the passing score up actually has the opposite effect of its intent: whereas the intent is to set a rich target for students to meet, the effect is for everyone to lower their eyes to the test and determine how many more items students know they need to answer correctly as the basis for the change, placing the quality determination even more prominently right in the midst of the tested content.

Raising the difficulty level or the passing score on a test designed to operate passively in the background makes it an active participant in the process of educating students, and it focuses the system well outside of and external to what should actually be happening in a classroom. Success in either case is well outside the goals of the education reform movement.

FEATURE #3: ADAPTIVE TESTING

Adaptive testing is a very elegant form of a standardized test without the limits of a nonadaptive test. Most notably, it allows for the most precise estimate of achievement possible in a testing environment, regardless of ability. The test *adapts* to the student, so that regardless of whether the student is years above or behind his or her peers, the test will "meet" them where they are in the process of providing a test score.

Consider that for a subject like reading, the ideal test would be one that contained the entire spectrum of achievement within that domain. Such a test would need to contain items that the lowest-performing students at the earliest grade level tested would barely be able to answer correctly, all the way up to items that the highest-performing high school students would struggle with.

That range of items should be able to capture the achievement levels of virtually every student somewhere between those two points. Of course, such a test would be thousands of items long and take weeks to administer, making standardized testing even more unpopular than it already is.

In a nonadaptive environment, a test designer has to select a subset of those items appropriate to the students to be tested, which is most often a grade level. The designer picks the items that will do the best job showing the distribution within the target population. That means that the test designer is going to have to forge a compromise between the amount of time available for the test and maximizing the amount of useful information that can be gleaned regarding the maximum number of students.

Most of those compromises occur at the high and low extremes within a grade level, since relatively few students occupy those positions. That means that for students that perform at the extremes, their scores are certainly less precise estimates than would be ideal. The major constraint within such tests, then, is that the amount of precision in the estimate depends (to a degree) on where a score ends up.

An adaptive test isn't subject to those constraints. Students enter an adaptive test environment, and the answers they provide shape the form of the test. A correct answer leads to a more difficult item, while an incorrect answer leads to an easier item, until the test can zero in on a point at which the answers above it are being answered incorrectly and the answers below it are being answered correctly.

That point becomes the student's score. The test will have adapted itself to the student in order to provide the best possible estimate of achievement for that student. In such an environment, virtually all students can receive a more precise estimate of their achievement than in a nonadaptive environment, since the test optimized itself to the student.

Certain forms of adaptive testing existed prior to computers, but with the introduction of a rich computing environment it has come into its own in recent years. Several states now use the model for their accountability tests, the National Assessment of Educational Progress (NAEP) has explored using it for the mathematics portion of their assessments, and commercially available adaptive tests have taken their place alongside the more traditional grade-level tests.

The advantages of adaptive testing are numerous. For example, no matter where a student is along the continuum of items, an equally precise estimate can be made regarding their achievement level, even when the student is several years ahead of or behind his or her peers. Nonadaptive tests cannot do that.

In addition, it generally requires less time than a nonadaptive test, is simpler to administer, and since it is computerized it presents the material to students in the medium that most modern students spend most of their time using anyway.

It is highly likely that within the next ten years adaptive testing will be the dominant form of standardized testing. Those responsible for building some of the standardized tests that will measure the Common Core are moving in that direction, and as more and more testing comes online the old way of doing things will become less and less appealing.

What we must not forget is that an adaptive test is still based upon the distributive paradigm and that all the warnings regarding accountability and standardized tests still apply. The test is still instructionally insensitive and should not be used to drive instruction, and all results are estimates and proxies only and not a direct measure of anything.

If accountability is applied to such tests, it will be entirely possible to reach an understanding as to what items in the continuum represent the passing scores and use those points as the focus for instruction.

If that happens, it will be harder to see and to understand, but the success determination will be just as firmly embedded in a test score as it is today, with all the accompanying risks of assigning the accountability determination to a standardized test.

FEATURE #4: VALUE-ADDED MODELS

One of the criticisms that policymakers have actually listened to regarding the test-based accountability model is that it holds schools and teachers accountable for things that happened before the student ever entered their school or classroom. That, by any stretch of the imagination, isn't fair. What policymakers and researchers have since attempted to do is determine the amount of growth a student experiences in a school or classroom during each year of schooling and hold the school accountable for that growth. That certainly, at least on the surface, sounds much more fair.

The idea of value-added work stems from the notion that for each person—or student, since we are talking about education—where choices for an environment exist, one of those choices will be more optimal than the rest. Value-added approaches would suggest that the optimal environment among the choices is the one in which the student is most likely to be able to maximize his or her own performance.

If a student had the option of different schools and classrooms, the idea behind the methodology is that each of those options and the individual student could be analyzed such that the optimal environment for that student could be found. Lots of variables are considered in such an analysis,[1] and performing such calculations generally requires a fairly extensive background in statistics.

As is the case with so many things in education, a tool that had and still has so much potential for optimizing performance has been turned on its head to a purpose beyond the original design. Remember that prereform policymakers saw that good schools did well on standardized tests and failed to understand that what they were looking at was a correlation. They then turned the tests into a cause, reversing the cause-and-effect sequence, with the logic that seemed to say: if good schools do well on such tests, and we want all schools to be good, all schools need to do well on such tests.

That logic makes no sense. The schools weren't doing well *because* they earned high test scores, the high test scores were a correlative to what the students in those schools had learned. If policymakers wanted what was happening in those schools to happen everywhere, then that is what they should have mandated. They should have realized that a high-achieving school will likely have a correlative in high test scores, but that a high test score on its own may or may not have a correlative with the goals of education.

That same logic is being applied in the use of value-added models to judge schools and teachers. A model that is quite elegant in its ability to identify an optimal environment in which a student can learn had to first know something about the type of growth experienced in each environment for similar students—otherwise you would have no basis for determining the optimal environment for the student.

Where it goes a bit backward is that a teacher capable of teaching in an optimized fashion for a particular type of student was doing something in order for that to happen—or if the teacher struggled with a particular type of student they likely weren't doing the things they needed to in order to cause good things to happen. The point is that the idea of value-add had to do with what schools and teachers were or were not doing, with test scores and all the other data points as passive observers of the process.

The idea was to identify what was and was not optimal for particular students so that successful environments could be replicated and scaled, and students could be placed in an environment that maximized their opportunity for success.

Holding a teacher or a school accountable for the growth on a passive measure does the exact same thing as assuming that a high test score can "cause" a school to be great—it removes the decisions and the activities that produced the conditions being seen through the lens of the measure as evidence that something good had happened and relegates those decisions and activities to a secondary position.

It suggests that what is important is the growth on the measure, when what it meant to do was suggest that what is important are the decisions that were made in the process of creating an optimal learning environment. That message gets lost in translation, and the measure winds up taking center stage.

Of course, the fact that standardized test scores are the principal source for the new value-added accountability attempts adds to the muddle. And since tests now serve as a primary driver of curriculum, whatever analysis emerges from test scores that aren't measuring what they purport to be measuring runs the risk that the value-add models will simply tell us what amount of tested content the student learned.

Locating success in a value-added measure means that success is no longer about finding the optimal environment in which to educate a particular student. Rather, success is once again positioned in a measurement tool designed for an entirely different set of purposes, none of which is commenting upon the quality of the effort by a teacher or school.

FEATURE #5: EQUITY

The idea of education reform was to ensure that every student, regardless of gender, race, socioeconomic status, or disability, was given every opportunity to achieve at very high levels. Success in the reform movement had to include—and did—the idea that all really did mean all, and that our sketchy history regarding disparate educational outcomes needed to change.

What can standardized tests, as the basis for the accountability package, contribute to that conversation?

The answer is much less than anyone imagined.

A standardized test is constructed to provide a statistical approximation of the status quo regarding achievement as well as a school or student's relative position within it, but not judge the underlying status quo that may be responsible for educational disparities. That is a mouthful.

Test designers go to great lengths to ensure that the tests do not discriminate against any particular group, and they have a whole series of statistics that they run on top of test data to eliminate items that behave inappropriately.

The point of the test is to show the distribution of students that is reflective of how things are achievement wise. If the world is racist or sexist, the underserved populations represented in those groups are likely to perform at a lower level than those in the majority, but the test results need to show any differences as differences in achievement only regardless of the particular cause.

If a set of test scores is examined and it is determined that one group of students is performing at a lower level than another, that cannot be because the items were easier for the majority population to answer or harder for the minority population to answer, given the unique experiences of both. It must be because of differences in performance, and nothing else.

An example unrelated to socioeconomic status can show how this occurs. When building items for a set of national assessments, test developers know that there are certain subjects that need to be avoided, such as snow and billboards. Those may seem strange choices, but for many children in the south snow is not something with which they have direct experience, and four states have laws prohibiting billboards: Alaska, Hawaii, Maine, and Vermont.

For a child that has never traveled outside of a land-locked state like Alaska, or an island state like Hawaii, or a student that has never left a nonbillboard state and knows of billboards only in the abstract, they would be disadvantaged when trying to answer a test item that had to do with billboards or snow.

This isn't some sort of political correctness gone awry, but a statistical reality. Students that lack familiarity with snow and/or billboards (most of Hawaii gets the double whammy here) do worse on items that reference them than students who are familiar with such things. A test designer would weed out such items because they interfere with what the test is trying to do. It is not trying to identify differences due to culture or where someone lives, but differences in achievement. Anything that gets in the way of that is just noise and needs to be eliminated to make the test fair.

Such weeding out is necessary so that when standardized test scores show disparities between various zip codes we can say—with a high degree of surety—that the differences may be due to any number of things, one of which may well be the bias in society, not due to a bias in the test.

The statistical processes that are applied when building a test are very good at separating out those issues so that the items that remain are fair for everyone regardless of where a person lives or the manner in which a person was raised. Getting rid of that sort of bias is important so that the score a student earns is as accurate an estimate as can be obtained from the test.

But while the scores may combine to offer an objective look at the status quo in terms of achievement, the status quo in terms of reality itself is rife with the whole gamut of what is currently unfair in the world. The goal is to create tests such that students who perform poorly do so because they performed poorly and not because the test was biased against them.

However, the reason for the poor performance may very well be because they are part of an underserved minority group or poor and did not answer as many questions correctly as their majority counterparts because they lacked similar opportunities. For the test to work it has to give everyone a fair shake, and having done so it can then help to identify the underlying injustices that might exist due to poverty and a host of other factors. The tests, in other words, need to be fair in order to offer a sense of an unfair status quo in which schools operate.

A question that may seem philosophical but is in fact very real is this: what are the consequences for having selected an instrument that has been carefully and uniquely designed to show a statistical approximation of the status quo regarding achievement as the primary tool of accountability?

However fair the instrument is in making its estimations regarding achievement, the achievement it identifies reflects all the unfairness that is a part of our modern society. We risk a real contradiction having selected such an instrument as the basis for accountability: a test that is designed to passively show such disparity isn't designed to help us resolve the disparity.

If we can make progress on alleviating the socioeconomic disparity and achievement follows, a standardized test will still show a distribution, but the disparity in that distribution will be based on something else. In other words, a standardized test instrument—in the hands of a thoughtful researcher—is actually a reasonable tool for helping us understand the degree to which the nature of the disparity changes over time.

But as an accountability tool, a standardized test is astonishingly shortsighted. Remember that a standardized test says nothing about educational quality—by design. It cannot comment upon its cause or any reason for a change.

It cannot say if a low score is the result of an impoverished school, or what the next step should be if the school wants to experience success. It cannot tell a high-performing school what to do to maintain its standing. If it did comment on educational quality, it would no longer be a fair test because now the scores would say something about a school being "good" or "bad," and any such correlation to such judgments has been carefully and painstakingly removed so that the test can be free of such bias.

It can show a distribution of students within a domain, and that is it. The reasons for why a school or a student lands at some point in the distribution are completely external to the measure.

Since it cannot comment upon educational quality, it stands to reason that a standardized test doesn't have anything to do with educational quality—and it doesn't. It has to do with providing a sense of how things are at a moment in time such that a student or a school can see where they stand in relation to everyone else.

If we make the monumental mistake of assuming that the tests are measures of educational quality, in that instant we change the meaning of the test from one that reflects the status quo to one that tells us that schools at the bottom are bad and schools at the top are good. Since a ranking of schools will generally reflect the socioeconomic condition of those schools, we are effectively suggesting that a quality school is one with a particular socioeconomic makeup.

In addition, assuming that test scores say something about educational quality has the very devious effect of creating differentiated expectations for schools based upon where students fall within the overall distribution. As a result, a standards movement that was supposed to set up a similar set of expectations for all students now in fact sets a differentiated standard for each school that risks leaving the status quo pretty much intact.

To make this as clear as possible, let's imagine a thirty-item test. I have mentioned several times that each of those items would be selected for inclusion because roughly half of the students will answer each of them incorrectly. In the end, however, some of those items will actually turn out to be easier or more difficult than the others. In some instances 60 percent or so of students will answer an item correctly, meaning it is a relatively easy item, and in others only 40 percent of students will answer correctly, meaning it would be a more difficult item.

This range allows us to line the items up from the easiest item all the way up to the most difficult. Once we have lined those items up in that fashion, we can then count from the bottom until we hit the passing score—let's say passing is set at twenty correct—and draw a line at that point.

What we can infer from that exercise is that a student who scores right at the passing score has a reasonably high probability of answering the items below the line correctly and a reasonably low probability of answering the items above the line incorrectly. Note that I said *probability*.

In reality kids can get to that passing score via lots of different scoring patterns across the full range of items, but overall it will still be true that for a student that just barely passes, the items above that point will be more likely to be missed, and the items below it will be more likely to be answered correctly.

This same pattern would be true at any of the score points, with a lower probability of a correct answer above the earned score and a higher probability below the earned score. (This is a pattern that is actually checked by a test designer to ensure that it holds. For example, items that a majority of high-achieving students answer incorrectly but that low-achieving students answer correctly are jettisoned. These items show a type of *reverse discrimination* that runs counter to the purpose of the test.)

If the test serves as the proxy it is designed to be, then these thirty items operate passively in the background, and other than those of us with pointy heads who do this sort of thing for a living, no one really cares about the process that went into their selection.

The process of ensuring that the test is operating fairly requires us to see that it doesn't make any judgments regarding whatever it is that contributes to a student earning a particular score. If it does—if poor-performing students all answer an item correctly but high-performing students miss it—it may be due to a curricular difference between high- and low-performing schools (or any one of a number of things), and thus we weed it out.

Placing accountability directly on those thirty items changes everything, from the test serving as a proxy for a domain that is referenced by the test to something else entirely. Every item is suddenly presumed to be meaningful, to have something to do with educational quality, or to offer advice regarding the curriculum that was taught.

But every single item that risked such a bias has been weeded out. Every item is now presumed to be able to say something regarding instruction when the criteria for selecting an item ensures that it will be curriculum independent. Items selected because they offered a proxy to schools in the form of a distribution now serve to define success.

Placing the success determination in those items means that once a school has a score the next step is to advance along the continuum of scores to attempt to answer a few more items correctly next year than this year. That in turn creates different expectations for a school depending on where a school falls along the continuum. Schools that average ten correct answers need to get to eleven and then twelve. A twelve school needs to try for thirteen and fourteen, and so it goes. And the idea isn't to get to the most challenging content on the test, since for a lot of the students that may not be considered to be reasonable, but to get to the next item, and then the next, and so on.

The fact that the test has a passing score in it adds another level of differentiation. Schools above that score are actually freed from the requirement to move from, say, twenty-two to twenty-three. Since the test declared them as a good school, they can continue to do what they were doing since it seems to have worked so far. They are free to set goals and make plans outside and *beyond* the test—they are freed from its constraints.

Schools below the passing score have a very different focus thrust on them. Their goals are *within* the test: moving the students along the continuum so that one day at some point in the future they, too, can get to the passing score.

Think about how far that is from a reform agenda, in which the idea is to have the same expectations for all kids. It allows us to say that at some future point we hope to have the same expectation, but not today. Today the job of a low-scoring school is to raise those scores, while the job of a high-scoring school is something else entirely.

Placing accountability in a distributive test instrument designed to provide a reflection of the status quo and then assigning different expectations based on where a school falls means that the lower in the distribution you are the lower the expectation, while the higher you are the higher the expectation. And it means that the assignment of an expectation is based on the current socioeconomic status of a school, with the poorest schools being assigned the lowest expectations.

What it does, to be blunt, is to reify the socioeconomic differences in the status quo rather than serve as a reasonable tool that can help schools break the cycle of poverty. It preserves the very thing reform was supposed to fix, leaving a zip code as the thing most likely to determine the expectations that await students and teachers.

That is why the best way to improve a school's standing in the current system is to change its demographics. Remember that the unfairnesses in society are not the basis on which the tests were built, but rather, the tests are designed to reflect the status quo. If the status quo is unfair—and it is—and you use that instrument to separate schools into categories of good and bad, you cannot help but apply those same labels to the socioeconomic condition of a school.

If you want to improve a school's standing in such a scenario, the socioeconomic conditions in which it operates has to be fixed.

Standardized testing is a marvelous tool when properly used. Early in my career I had a chance to have dinner with one of the pioneers of many of the statistical processes and applications used to make such tests fair for all students, and he told me that he could not count the number of times that he received letters from students who had taken one of his exams that showed them performing against type and how that was the only way the school took notice.

Some were poor or minority students whose social standing prevented educators from seeing their potential, while others were kids perceived as somewhat odd or socially distant but who clearly wanted to learn and weren't being noticed.

He also pointed out to me how often jocks and athletes or other popular students actually struggled with academics but were afraid of the stigma of seeking help, and yet when they had an honest sense of where they stood they sought that help out. Some students that were expected to struggle or succeed certainly did so, and the test scores served as an impetus to find meaningful ways to help. His point was simply that having a sense of how a student or a school stacks up against the world could be a very helpful data point.

But it is not a statement on quality. It says nothing about whether the student is a good or a bad student; it doesn't comment on the quality of the school or the socioeconomic makeup of the student. Outside of the test score students are all those things, and their combination will contribute to a student's level of achievement, but a test score is about achievement, independent of that environment.

Fast-forward twenty-plus years from that dinner and the picture is clouded. The quality judgment is now located directly within the standardized tests students take each school year that were not designed for such a purpose and, to my knowledge, no magic wand has been waved that can magically change that fact. However sophisticated the analysis or the approach, placing the quality determination in a test is a monumental mistake.

The impact of that inappropriate judgment is most heavily felt in the schools that have historically struggled. That to me is the most shameful part of this experiment.

A gesture intended to ensure that all students could learn to very high standards in fact allows those who were already doing so to continue on their merry way, while offering a very low bar to those who historically struggled, with a change in demographics as the best way out of that predicament.

The point of reform was to ensure that all kids had a chance, and that point is not now a requirement in the system. Success in the current system is a far cry from the successes that were imagined by those that put the system in place.

NOTE

1. Value Added Research Center website, http://varc.wceruw.org/, accessed April 11, 2013.

III

The Next Generation of Change: Moving Away from an Unfit Fitness

Kenneth Burke describes an interesting phenomenon in his book *Permanence and Change* called "trained incapacity," which describes perfectly the situation in which we find ourselves today regarding much that happens in education. I quote below at length, as he does a far better job of saying it than I can. Regarding the natives of some theoretical island, he points out the following:

> Because their Christian missionary and doctor wore a raincoat during storms, they linked raincoats with rainy weather, and accordingly begged him to don the raincoat as medicine against drought. Irrigation would have been a more effective means, yet their attempts to coerce the weather by homeopathic magic were not "escapist" in the restricted sense. They were a faulty selection of means due to a faulty theory of causal relationships. [1]

Burke finishes his thought a page later:

> One adopts measures in keeping with past training—and the very soundness of this training may lead him to adopt the wrong measures. *People may be unfitted by being fit in an unfit fitness* (my italics). [2]

It is a simple truth that we now revere a system of education that cannot achieve the goals it purports to embrace. Someone once saw that high standardized test scores seemed to go hand in hand with good schools and assumed a causal relationship. It was no different in logic than associating a raincoat with the ability to make it rain.

In previous chapters I have attempted to show several of the most fundamental components of the current educational system in terms of what they were designed to do versus what policymakers and others hoped they might become simply by declaring it so. I have tried to show how illogical it is to demand that something produce a result that is completely beyond and often antithetical to the actual design. And I have attempted to show how the manner in which we talk about education has masked and obscured much of this, making it difficult to see and even more difficult to discuss.

The combined result of the decisions made regarding these components is to create a system that is at conflict with what it is attempting to do. Consider the following that have already been presented in this book:

1. Standards based on a behavioral model exist to constrain, control, and limit what happens in a classroom, not free people to find new ways to excel and succeed in an ever-changing world.
2. All students must succeed on a test that requires some to not do so well in order for the system to work. A standardized test is not something designed to allow all students to perform at the upper end— some by design will not.
3. The quality determination in schools has been assigned to a tool that by design says nothing about the quality of a school.
4. A standardized test is designed to say nothing about specific curricular changes that need to be made in a school, and yet educational policy positions it as a primary source for informing such decisions.
5. The decisions a teacher makes are judged via an instrument designed to be independent of those decisions.
6. The test content is now the de facto curriculum, invalidating the test results wherever that is the case, which is anywhere the test content now serves as the de facto curriculum.
7. Invalid test scores now serve as the basis for much of the quality determination in schools.
8. If the status quo is the initial point of comparison for a research tool, and you make the research tool the basis for everything that you do, you risk miring yourself in whatever the current state of things looks like.
9. In a system such as that described in #8, you risk working harder than you ever have in your life to preserve the very thing you are trying to change.
10. The goal of having the same expectation for all students is immediately squashed when the success determination against that goal is made

as of a date certain each year with an instrument designed to show the differences in a population. The choice to do it as of a date certain each year preserves the historical unfairness in the status quo as of that date, meaning that historically top-performing schools will "succeed" and be freed to do what they want, while low-performing schools will "fail" and must focus on test scores, which in turn risks leaving them ensconced in their historically vulnerable position.

The notion of trained incapacity is very much at work here. We associate several versions of the raincoat—behavioral standards, standardized tests, and imprecise terminology that very few bother to check—with the ideas of quality schools, success for all, and a sense of an overall mission for education, when none of those things has a causal link to any of the desired outcomes.

What has been created is a set of associations with an idea that actually represents an "unfit fitness," a cure for what ails us that makes things worse under the guise that it can make things better. As we train our students in such an environment—and as our teachers struggle to help students in that environment—we risk setting them up for what is without a doubt an unfit fitness. True success in that environment is, in fact, anything but.

If all we did was remove the incommensurability from the system—those things that are at odds with each other and that fight one another in producing quality outcomes—we could improve the system of education as it stands by leaps and bounds.

NOTES

1. Kenneth Burke, *Permanence and Change: An Anatomy of Purpose* (Berkeley and Los Angeles: University of California Press, 1954), 9.
2. Burke, *Permanence and Change*, 10.

Chapter Nine

Fomenting the Right Changes

Lots of systems exist that are designed to help organizations work through the process of change. These go by names such as *strategic planning*, or the more recent (and rather helpful) version called *theory of change*, and they are extremely useful in plotting out how best to create change—particularly in communities such as education that have a wide variety of stakeholders and participants.[1]

My concern here is not with the approach to fomenting a desired change, but rather in determining the types of changes that need to be made. It will be deeply unsatisfactory to leave the system of schooling as it currently stands in place. Thus I will argue for a type of change and leave the methodology to others.

True to a claim in an earlier chapter that declaring a system broken results in introducing lots of inefficiencies into the process of "fixing" something, I don't wish to suggest that education is a broken system in need of being replaced, but rather, that it requires a different set of improvements than it has historically tolerated.

These improvements need to relate to how we organize the system of education, and we need to be willing to see the educational system quite differently than what we have in the past, such that it becomes commensurate with a current set of goals and objectives.

If we are to do that, we need a methodology for understanding what type of structure will in fact be commensurate with the goals of education that can then be delivered through a strategic planning methodology. Given that education is a monolith of enormous proportions, moving it toward something different will have to begin with where we find ourselves at the present and yet still be able to morph into a desired future state.

Any attempt to invent a new system of education from the ground up is not likely to get very far.

What is needed is a strategy for systems change designed for an environment where the givens are in fact not changeable and yet that can foment excellence both because of and in spite of that rigidity. Several years ago I discovered a workable strategy for doing just that, but it comes from a place far removed from education and the world of social change.

Eli Goldratt is a famous business writer that writes extensively about how systems work and how to find ways to constantly improve them. Goldratt introduced the idea that the limits in a system are generally the result of a small number of constraints that have a profound effect on the system as a whole.

He then offers what has long been seen as a unique approach to address those constraints once they have been identified: to actually organize the entire system around them, effectively removing them as constraints by making them the focus of the system, which in turn offers a meaningful improvement. (I'll explain this more in a minute.)

Goldratt's ideas are powerful for education because the primary source for his theories is a factory—something that is as recalcitrant in its ability to swap out the various parts and pieces as education. I want to be very clear that I am in no way equating the process of manufacturing a widget with the process of educating a student.

Rather, I have discovered that the systems that support both respond to change in similar ways. In both it is very hard to substitute one process for another, or to skip a step or a process, or to gather an objective viewpoint that takes in the entire process. Both are made up of very complicated parts and pieces that must interact with each other in order to accomplish the task at hand, and both are run within systems that require constant attention and need to be constantly improved.

Goldratt's approach to systems change extends nicely to educational systems because we must be successful with the parts and pieces we have now and do not have the luxury of declaring that things will get better if we could just change out a part of the system. In fact, Goldratt has a very interesting strategy for how to handle the parts to the system that really should be swapped out for something better but cannot for any number of reasons.

A *constraint* to Goldratt is anything that gets in the way of the goal of an organization. In education a constraint would be anything that prevented the system of education from achieving its goal of educating all students to a very high level. Educators and policymakers by their actions have assumed that lots of things qualify as constraints, such as low test scores, large class size, lack of educational or common standards, poor teacher quality, socioeconomic conditions, Algebra II, and a host of things almost too numerous to mention.

In fact, there would appear on first blush to be so many constraints that it would be impossible to know where to even begin, which makes it very difficult to prioritize among them, and indeed in education knowing what to prioritize is a huge part of the challenge.

Here is one area where Goldratt's approach can offer the field of education some insights. He suggests that any system in fact has only a few constraints, although in any system an uncritical look will make it appear as if constraints are everywhere. He readily acknowledges that it is very difficult to identify the real constraints and separate those out from what are actually nonconstraints.

Find the actual constraints, Glodratt argues, and removing them as constraints will then move many of the nonconstraints to a manageable position and show that they aren't the constraints they once seemed to be. It doesn't dismiss or reduce the importance of the nonconstraints, but rather it allows us to see them in their proper perspective.

It's what you do with a constraint once you identify it that I find so interesting in Goldratt's philosophy. Rather than manage around it or heap resources onto it (he calls this *expediting*, and it's only to be done as a last resort), you instead organize the entire system around it so that it loses its ability to serve as a constraint. If some process is gumming up the works, you ask what sort of an organization would need to exist such that the process is no longer a problem, even to the point of letting that process dictate the pace at which the rest of the system can work.

Consider an example of what it might look like to organize a system around a constraint if we apply the idea to education. Time, for example, is a potential constraint when it comes to learning. Some students learn more quickly than others, and that can differ subject by subject, grade by grade, and certainly student by student.

In the current system, the amount of time available for learning is essentially the same for each student and grade, which is based upon the implicit assumption that all students will have sufficient time to learn the material given the appropriate instruction. If that is not the case (and it's pretty clear that it is not), then time could be considered as a potential constraint to meeting the goal.

The difference in Goldratt's approach to such a constraint versus what we normally do is that he insists that in order to remove it as a constraint you must organize the entire system around it, rather than try to manage around it. Managing around as opposed to organizing around it would require schools to offer some additional time to students who needed it through an extended school day, or to allow those progressing at a more rapid pace to move ahead a grade or to an advanced class, which is exactly what we do now—we *expedite* the process.

Expediting doesn't solve the problem in a sustainable way, but it requires instead additional resources and effort, putting the solution at risk should those resources dry up. The process of expediting is exactly the manner in which we attempt to solve the vast majority of problems in education, and it is built directly into a rather large amount of our educational policy.

Organizing the system *around* the constraint of time looks profoundly different. It would require that proficiency become the driver for the amount of time a student needs to learn to a specified level, making the time it takes to achieve proficiency the metric, not the level of proficiency obtained in some specified amount of time.

If the system is organized around the possible constraint of time, lots of other things that appeared to be constraints may no longer function as constraints, such as the failure to earn a high standardized test score as of a date certain each year, or the amount of seat time required for a diploma. It isn't that these things just up and disappear, but rather, they are relegated to a position as something other than a constraint.

Consider that absent Goldratt's approach those of us in education are left with the only option being to manage around or expedite what appears to be a whole gamut of constraints: the socioeconomic status of a student or school, the demand for higher test scores, the standards as they currently exist, and others.

In addition, researchers have pointed out lots of what appear to be additional constraints that are now also expedited: children coming to school ready to learn in kindergarten, students leaving school ready to enter the worlds of college and work, Algebra II as a gateway to being able to apply for college, and so it goes.

If any of these really is a constraint, then the only way to remove it as a constraint is to organize the rest of the system around it. If all we do is attempt to manage around the constraint—which is what we do now—we can only accomplish the task with additional resources and effort. If we take Goldratt's approach, we would imagine what the system would look like if we organized the system such that it removed the status of the thing as a constraint.

Such an exercise then allows us to ask if the thing really is a constraint on the goal. It allows us to see if removing the thing as a constraint—but not removing it from the system which would be illogical for something that is considered to be a constraint—moves the entire system closer to its goal.

If it only improves the ability of the thing to make its contribution, then it probably isn't an actual constraint on the system. If it improves the ability of the system to meet its goals, which involves relegating many of the former constraint candidates to nonconstraint status, then the thing is likely a constraint and organizing the system around it will remove its constraint status.

In that sense, many things that are treated like constraints in the present system will lose their constraint status if they exist in a different system. They will still exist, but they won't mean what they once did. They may still represent a painful process or activity, but they will no longer be in the way of the goal of education, which is clearly defined in 2013 as helping all students achieve at a high level commensurate with college and/or workplace success by the completion of high school. [2]

Here is the most remarkable thing to me about such an approach: *It allows us to properly position the socioeconomic status of a school or a student as a nonconstraint.* Think about that. We know that the socioeconomic status of a school is one of the most powerful indicators for whether or not the students in that school will eventually participate in the end goal of education. An uncritical look at the system would insist that the socioeconomic status of a school or student is therefore a massive constraint. However, schools cannot be organized in such a way that the socioeconomic status of a student can be made not to matter. It does and will always matter.

In addition, if we attempted to organize schools in such a fashion (by the way, forced busing in the 1960s and 1970s was a gesture designed to address this constraint, just to put a very real face on what it might look like), what we discover is that unlike organizing around the constraint of time very few if any of the other potential constraints disappear. In fact, organizing such that socioeconomic status is equalized across schools shows that for the purpose of organizing schools that socioeconomic status is not a true constraint, as not much changes in terms of the ability of a school to maximize student performance against the goal.

Saying that socioeconomic status is not a constraint around which the system should be organized in no way means that we assume it doesn't exist, or that it isn't important, but rather that if we choose those things that are actually constraints and build the system around them then perhaps poverty need not be a primary predictor of a student's educational outcome.

Consider again my example of time as a constraint, and consider how socioeconomic status fits into a system that could organize itself around the constraint of time. In that system it would be highly likely that it would take more time, energy, and expertise to educate students in our poorest schools to an appropriate level of proficiency, but since time has specifically been removed as a constraint the point is to take the time necessary to ensure that each student succeeds.

And it removes a one-size-fits-all approach, which stands an excellent chance of aligning the right resources with the right students, which is important since such a policy—just like any policy in education—is unlikely to be accompanied by more money. Doing so would put more students closer to the goal of achieving at a very high level than the current system that is constrained by time, and yet come close to achieving that goal.

But most importantly, organizing a school such that time is removed as a constraint gives poverty nonconstraint status. Doing so doesn't alleviate poverty, but it also doesn't require a fix for what ails society in order for the system to function. Rather, the system stands a chance of functioning effectively and moving more students toward the goal in spite of whatever their socioeconomic status might be. That is a powerful idea.

When things that appear by any reasonable person to be constraints on the system can be moved to a nonconstraint role simply by organizing a system around the real constraints, you have a chance at real and meaningful change.

This is where the role of practical measurement needs to enter the picture. The purpose of our measurement systems in schools has for far too long been in the form of standardized test scores by which we judge the quality of the school, which as has been repeatedly noted is not something a test score can tell you.

Again, a Goldratt sentiment is helpful: the role of measurement in a system, he says, is to "induce the parts to do what's good for the organization as a whole."[3] What is good for the organization as a whole is that it meets its goal.

If that goal is educating all students to a very high level, then the parts of the system need to work together to do that, with the measurement system helping to identify where the constraints exist. That way the system can be organized such that those things no longer function as constraints.

The measurement system needs to help identify the things that hinder or prevent the achievement of the goal, so that the types of change that need to be made are clear. Most importantly, however, is that the measurement system assist in separating out the actual constraints and nonconstraints regarding the goal. Organizing around a nonconstraint creates frustration and inefficiency, while organizing around an actual constraint renders the nonconstraints to a manageable status.

In that vein we can ask a really tough question as to whether our present system of schooling is organized around constraints or nonconstraints when it comes to the goal of educating all students to a very high level. That may perhaps offer some impetus for improvements if we discover that the current system runs counter to the goal.

So let's ask the question: Since the two most basic organizational principles for our schools are based on the constraints of geography and age-based grade assignment, are these constraints that if organized around will help move the system closer to the goal? The answer is a resounding no.

That both are a practical response to organizing and managing something as large and as complex as the education of fifty-five million students is true, but when it comes to the goal they have little to do with it beyond gathering the students together. If we don't attempt to think about the actual constraints that can be managed and organized around them, then we risk grade levels and the socioeconomic status that is inherent in geography as the predominant organizing principle in determining the general outcome of a school, since geography and grade levels are the primary means by which schooling is organized.

To put it another way, if we desire all our students to be able to be fully educated, then the system needs to acknowledge that it can only achieve that if it organizes itself around the actual constraints, which are those things that have the power to subsume the things we cannot control and frankly overwhelm them. If the system of education is to be brought in line with its goal, then the current manner in which things are organized won't do. The present system is not designed to allow the goal for all students because it is organized around the wrong things.

For too long we have assumed that the idealism in an "all children can learn" approach is possible without a fundamental change in how the system of education is organized. No Child Left Behind (NCLB) insisted that all children would be great by 2014, with *great* defined as "on grade level," and before that Goals 2000 stated that by the year 2000 the state of education wouldn't be too far behind what NCLB mandated.

Both of them defined outcomes that were profoundly different than the status quo, and they then suggested that the means to doing so was effectively to try harder. This was because both actually enabled the organizing structure as it existed at the time and expected that structure to produce a different result. A different, more idealistic result is certainly possible, but it requires a different structure.

Researchers have identified a significant number of potential constraints that are in the way of the system of education accomplishing its goal. Consider the following:

1. Time to learn. Students learn at different rates and in different ways. Unless time is a variable we will always have differentiated performance, and the differences are likely to follow socioeconomic lines.
2. Age-based grade assignments. We assign students to grades by age, which reifies the idea that a student will have between twelve to thirteen years to master the content, with each year as a self-contained year.
3. College/workplace readiness. Researchers have pointed out that the worlds of high school and college and work are very far apart in terms of their expectations, making the transition that much more difficult.
4. Children entering school ready to learn. One of the greatest hindrances to young children making appropriate progress in schools has to do

with the skill sets young children bring to school. If young children lack those skills, it is very difficult to catch them up to their peers.

5. The loss of creativity in schools by middle school. Many have written about the death of creativity in schools by the middle grades and have pointed out both why that has happened and its impact on learning.
6. Boredom/lack of aspirations. Related to #5, school is considered by a great many students across the socioeconomic spectrum to be boring, and many students lack heroes or adults they can look to as role models, much to the detriment of their learning.
7. Geographic assignment of students to schools. Students attend schools that are in their neighborhoods, or when school choice exists in schools convenient to their parents' place of work, not necessarily the schools that are capable of serving the unique needs of each student.
8. Access to current technology. Access differs dramatically across the socioeconomic spectrum.
9. Attitudes toward the teaching profession. At present society tends to view teachers in a somewhat negative light, and most recent policy is such that it presumes teachers are a root cause of what ails education.
10. The lack of a proficiency-based educational system. Our goal is for all students to learn at very high levels, and yet the basis for much of our system is a standardized test, which is designed to show the differences within a population. These two approaches to education are severely at odds with one another.

If the list doesn't appear to be very original, that's because it isn't. All of these things have been viewed as constraints by any number of writers and researchers, and the list of those who have attempted to address the challenges presented by them is a long one.

What hasn't been done, however, is to attempt to treat each as a constraint in the manner Goldratt insists is the means by which a constraint could be relegated to nonconstraint status: organize the system around them. Each so far has been given attention that amounts to expediting, wherein an increased effort was made in an attempt to address the obvious shortcomings in the current system.

Oftentimes the effort was monumental, and I don't want to shortchange anyone who would commit a large portion of his or her professional life to these issues by suggesting they were wrong to expend effort in that way. Instead, what I do want to do is insist that if these are truly the constraints that are most in the way of the goal of educating all students to a very high level that they are worthy of a different sort of attention so that they no longer function as a constraint.

Let me be equally clear on another point: these are *potential* constraints, which means that as an organizing structure is envisioned for each, some will prove to be constraints, while others will no longer be seen as constraints but as something that can be managed within the new organizational structure.

Here are some things that need to be off the table as potential constraints, again, not because they don't exist, but because changing them isn't possible or likely and so organizing around them needs to be seen as counterproductive:

1. Poverty/socioeconomic status
2. Replacing the teaching force
3. Standardized test scores
4. School accountability programs

Ignoring any of these things is certainly not possible, but the point is that no good comes from organizing *around* them, since organizing around them does not remove any of them as a constraint to the goal of educating all students to a very high level.

We already organize schools around their socioeconomic status, and that hasn't gotten us anywhere. Replacing our teaching force is not possible or desirable, and I've droned on now for many pages regarding the dangers of organizing schools around testing or shortsighted policies. You could, should you choose, organize around any of these and probably see the metrics that were tied to each tick upward, but that improvement risks having little or nothing to do with the bigger goal.

Organizing around them in the vast majority of cases actually gets you further from the goal. Thus, they must not be treated as constraints, but as things that can be made manageable once the actual constraints are removed.

We can now tackle the question as to what a measurement system looks like that can help us understand where the constraints exist: we do what Goldratt insists we do when we look inside any system and identify the bottlenecks, the pieces and parts to the system causing things to get all gummed up.

The public education system that spans from kindergarten through grade twelve as a system is unique because it employs over twenty-five thousand[4] researchers and professionals doing work for the purpose of understanding and improving education. Everything on my list of potential constraints is backed up by a huge body of knowledge and research that is explicitly about the identification of constraints. A complete bibliography of peer-reviewed articles that have already identified the things on the list as potential constraints would stretch on for hundreds of pages.

In addition, much has been written regarding the structure of our school system and the need for something different, and yet the structure of our present school system hasn't changed much in the hundred or so years since the bulk of it was put in place. Lots of reasons exist for not changing, including the seemingly rational fear that any change could make things worse and not better, the power of inertia, and the difficulty in envisioning something different that doesn't represent a big one-off experiment.

What has long been missing in schools is a theory regarding what to change that can accommodate the political and practical realities that surround schooling while at the same time addressing the constraints that prevent schools from meeting their goals. The result of not having such a theory is an expedited approach to each problem, one that requires additional resources and effort to overcome the constraint but that doesn't change the system per se.

By not changing the system, the expedited approach means that when the resources dry up the system will experience a return to stasis without having created a better, more sustainable state of things.

Extending Goldratt's ideas to education should be of interest because it offers the means by which to foment change based on the plethora of educational research that points us in the direction of the goal of education. It doesn't ask anyone to work in a vacuum, nor does it assume that a policymaker needs to act first before a constraint can be rendered a nonconstraint.

Instead, the idea of a theory of constraints in schools begins with the premise that schools are complex, messy places that will always be messy and complex, and it ends with the notion that our goal is to constantly seek out the constraints that exist and then organize the system such that the constraint is reduced to a nonconstraint.

In that way, the improvements that our schools so desperately need can be put in place and can stick.

NOTES

1. The Aspen Institute and Act Knowledge are two leading proponents of theory of change. Both have excellent resources available for those who want to look at specific approaches to the types of changes discussed here.

2. This is the stated goal for the Common Core as well as the assessment consortia building assessments for the Common Core content areas of reading and math. In fact, one of the two assessment consortia is called PARCC, which is an acronym for Partnership for Assessment of Readiness for College and Careers.

3. Eliyahu M. Goldratt and Jeff Cox, *The Goal: A Process of Ongoing Improvement, Third Edition* (Great Barrington, MA: North River Press, 2004), 274.

4. The American Educational Research Association just announced that they have over twenty-five thousand paying members.

Chapter Ten

Cause and Effect and Inefficiencies

To return to Burke's analogy that opened this final section, raincoats do not cause rain, just as test scores and behavioral standards do not cause success. Nevertheless, the search for the perfect raincoat in education continues.

This is, on the one hand, understandable, since the system of education is an extremely complex one that tends to reveal only snippets of itself to the public, and these snippets tend to take on a larger-than-life role as a result, and thus they take on more meaning than they can actually handle. Test scores are just one example of this.

But while on the one hand it may be understandable, on the other, it is inexcusable. Elevating the few things that are recognizable to the majority of people to being the lens through which we will see and judge and shape education risks inefficiencies being introduced to the system, and it strains the logical boundaries of cause and effect.

I pointed out in the last chapter how organizing a system around its constraints can relegate those parts of the system to nonconstraint status, as well as show that a number of things that once appeared as constraints actually aren't constraints. This aligns with Goldratt's philosophy that any system will have only a few constraints but that an uncritical look can easily convince someone that there are in fact lots of constraints.

The critical look is necessary, because if you organize around a nonconstraint the result is inefficiency. In our search for the "perfect raincoat," we have indeed introduced a number of inefficiencies.

Those inefficiencies come in several different forms that then interfere with the cause-and-effect relationship of schools moving more students toward the goal (i.e., all students being educated to a very high level). The three most common forms of these inefficiencies in education are as follows:

1. Death by proxy, in which the idea that the educational quality of a school can be measured by a proxy is extended well beyond schooling and applied to the quality of a student's entire educational career, the quality of a teacher, the principal, and more.
2. Decontextualized interpretations, in which the assumption is that a measure will mean the same thing no matter who achieved it, where it was achieved, or the manner in which it was achieved.
3. The rich school fallacy, which occurs when we assume that the right model for all schools—poor schools especially—is for them to behave like rich schools.

In many cases, more than one is actually at work, confounding the issue even further.

Below I provide three examples of the search for the perfect raincoat that show what happens when you attempt to organize around nonconstraints, and the inefficiencies that result. I do so to point out that we are already willing to offer up new organizational structures within our schools, so moving forward the goal should be to pick those that are actually constraints, not just target what is convenient or politically expedient.

The good news in these examples is that we already have at least some sense of how to change. The bad news is that we seem to keep picking the wrong things.

ALGEBRA II

It was discovered some years back that students who entered college or held higher-paying jobs than their peers completed Algebra II at a much higher rate than those that did not.[1] It is noteworthy to point out that Algebra II is often a requirement on college applications, and a student planning to go on to college would know that (or their parents or counselors would) and opt for the course, and that those students would have been more likely to recognize the value in taking such a course.

Students who chose not to opt for the course were then, of course, behind their peers in terms of being prepared to apply for college, and they became part of the correlation that suggested they were likely to work in lower-paying jobs. Students who opted out of Algebra II would have to make up the course later in their high school career if college was to become an option or if they suddenly realized their education was missing something. Algebra II, then, was seen as a gatekeeper in that regard.

The policy response to this problem was to treat Algebra II as a constraint and insist that all students should take and pass Algebra II, thereby eliminating that barrier to college entrance (and possibly letting the correlation with higher-paying jobs come to bear on Algebra II takers) by organizing a part of high schools around it.

The decision to organize in this fashion was because the goal in their eyes was to increase the number of students applying for and being accepted to college, as well as those in higher-paying jobs. The motive for this is pretty pure—in a democratic educational system schools ought to do everything in their power to see that every student can maximize their opportunity for future success. No reasonable argument can be made against such a goal.

What someone was actually looking at, however, was a correlation that they assumed was in fact a causal connection. One causal connection certainly existed when it came to Algebra II: a student desiring to attend college was required to take the course, so that desire *caused* the selection of the course.

But the opposite could not then also be said to be logically true: taking Algebra II at no point in time represented a causal connection with a student applying to college. It certainly appeared that way. After all, any right-minded person looking at the data and seeing that the vast majority of those attending college opted for Algebra II, and the vast majority of those who opted out did not, makes a pretty compelling case for a causal connection. The same can be said when looking at salaries and then comparing that to Algebra II–taking practices.

But while taking Algebra II may mean you can check off one more box on the things you need to do to get ready to apply for college, the fact is that Algebra II does not cause students to want to apply for and attend college or earn a higher wage. Nevertheless, several significant groups assumed a causal relationship and therefore went to great lengths to see that the requirement was imposed on all students.

That way, they reasoned, that part of the pathway would be cleared and no longer stand as a barrier to college entrance or higher wages, with the ultimate desired cause being that more would apply for and attend college and earn a higher wage.

Only no one applied for and went to college *because* they had taken Algebra II. Students took Algebra II because they wanted to go to college. If you want to change the mind of someone from not wanting to or even thinking that they had a chance to attend college to wanting to attend college, you should attempt to persuade them that they can and should go to college. Forcing all students to take Algebra II is a rather shortsighted way to compel that to happen.

As to the salary piece, if a correlation exists between applying for college and Algebra II, then you will also most definitely see a correlation between higher wages and Algebra II, since college attendance also correlates with higher salaries. That one is pretty simple.

The way we can recognize the lack of constraint status of something like Algebra II is to first ask if organizing around it has moved us closer to the goal of educating all students to a very high level and if it allowed the system to become more efficient by allowing several things that once appeared to be constraints to be relegated to nonconstraint status. If it fails one or the other of those tests, then it would have been better to treat Algebra II as a nonconstraint—as something important, of course, but not as something that if organized around will make a school more efficient at moving more of its students toward the goal of education.

The requirement of Algebra II for all fails both tests and as a result produces inefficiencies as a result of applying the rich school fallacy and the failure to fully contextualize the decision. It fails on logic alone: students do not go to college because they took Algebra II, but rather, they take Algebra II as a prerequisite to applying for college.

The rich school fallacy here is that Algebra II does of course correlate with college attendance or higher salaries, but that correlation is accompanied by a host of other behaviors, and those other behaviors are disproportionately positioned in the wealthier schools and communities. Ignoring that fact means that passing Algebra II can be claimed to mean the same regardless of the relative wealth that surrounds a school, when the ability to have the desired correlations will still largely depend on a student's zip code.

What has happened is that it was assumed that the correlations that existed in a wealthy school could be made to appear in all schools regardless of the other contextualized issues that contribute to a student's decision to go to college and thus opt for Algebra II. By decontextualizing the issue, policymakers were able to suggest that what mattered when it came to getting into college was Algebra II, not the resources and supports that exist in disproportionate numbers as you move from poorer to wealthier communities.

Decontextualizing the issue enables the assumption that the correlation between Algebra II and college attendance is actually causal, which then allows a policymaker to believe they have done their jobs and get frustrated when the logic doesn't pan out because failure can be pushed onto those responsible for implementation.

Treating Algebra II as a constraint means that it risks becoming another raincoat, one that we asked kids to put on so that it would make it rain college students and higher wages, when no real causal connection between the two exists. This in no way implies that making Algebra II a requirement is a bad curricular decision or that it is unimportant—that criticism would need to be made by curriculum experts.

Rather, treating it as a constraint on students considering college or experiencing future success risks inserting inefficiencies into the system. In the theory of systems change being described here, that is a mistake, because it makes the system less effective at achieving its goal and more expensive to operate.

COLLEGE AND WORKPLACE READINESS IN A TEST SCORE

I mentioned in an earlier chapter that the case has been made that in addition to the goal of educating all students to a very high level it is now necessary that we also properly prepare them for the worlds of college and work, and who could argue with that as a goal? I want that for my own children, and it makes perfect sense.

The manner in which we are currently engaged in determining whether or not such goals have been met is one where all three inefficiencies are at work: death by proxy, decontextualized interpretations, and the rich school fallacy. All three come into play because the manner in which such readiness determinations are planning to be made will involve identifying some point on a standardized test in reading and math as the signal. That means that again a proxy risks being interpreted absent its context and that the response in poorer schools needs to be to mirror what happens in wealthier schools.

An example of this is in an application of Dave Conley's very fine work, which has been instrumental in pointing out that the work being done in high schools and the work being done during the freshman year in college are dramatically different, due in large part to the designs and purposes inherent in the different institutions.[2]

As the need for a college education has grown, that gap has become more and more obvious, and Conley has done an excellent job identifying what the skill sets are that students need to have in order to succeed in college that aren't a part of the high school curriculum. These include habits of mind, key content, academic behaviors, and contextual skills and awareness.

Among the specifics are the levels of numeracy and literacy that will be needed, along with things such as intellectual openness, inquisitiveness, reasoning, argumentation and proof, and precision and accuracy.[3]

Our answer to ensuring that students are going to leave high school prepared for the world of college as identified by Conley should be to ensure that those skills become an integral part of the curriculum, that teachers are trained in the various ways to teach them to the diverse array of their students, and that such training for things that fall into the category "habits of mind" also reaches to the middle schools to ensure that they are also doing their part.

We must also realize that many of those skills will come from students rubbing shoulders outside of school, and that the available resources for learning such extracurricular skills differ according to socioeconomic status.

While Conley's work has been well received, the vehicles by which policymakers intend to ensure it happens are standardized test scores in reading and math. They are, quite literally, looking at those tests and attempting to identify a point on them that signals college readiness as Conley identifies it.[4]

If even half of what I have argued to this point is true, then asking a test score to serve as such a signal should be seen as a preposterous thing. That determination must involve questions about all of the behaviors Conley identifies, not just the subject matter material. Attempts to ask tests of limited content to tell us when a student is ready to succeed at college or in the world of work will place that determination within a small segment of two domains, when the actual requirement goes well beyond that.

The same tests that serve as the quality indicator for the entire school now are being asked to serve as an indicator for all of a student's years of study and preparation to that point, and even more, as a predictor of future success, since the quality determination for readiness is based upon some desired future state.

The search for the perfect raincoat here is that high test scores—based as they are upon an overall distribution of how things happen to be at a moment—fairness, unfairness, and all—will identify those students at the top of the heap as those who are most likely to go and be successful (a nice little research project could be designed and conducted that would show just that).

Assuming that success is commensurate with those high test scores means that the success is then not seen for what it is—a socioeconomic phenomenon. Rather, that test score is seen as somehow having a causal connection to a desired future state, one so powerful that as other students also achieve that score that it will then mean the same for a socially disadvantaged student as it does the rich kids.

Students who are likely to have a good chance at eventual success are more likely to have been given the chance to develop all those other skills Conley identifies, meaning that for those students the high test scores correlate with the presence of such skills.

But correlations are not causal. The test scores did not cause those high-performing students to develop the other skills, just as the presence of those skills did not cause those test scores. Both were a result of something else, but for high-performing students living under somewhat privileged conditions I think it is fair to say that high test scores and the presence of those skills would likely show a correlation, a correlation that exists because of the underlying socioeconomic conditions for those students.

That same test score risks meaning something very different for a student learning under very different conditions, meaning that in the absence of the context that difference may be difficult to see and understand. If a student in a lower socioeconomic environment lacked the chance to learn many of those other skills and spent his or her time learning in a school that was at risk of closing lest the test scores be increased, success risks being placed in those test scores and nowhere else.

A teach-to-the-test mentality may well allow the student to grind out a similar test score, but of course it won't mean anything, and it certainly won't correlate to the other skills Conley identifies. That score, for those students, will say nothing about whether that student has been properly prepared for future greatness. Absent that larger context, the danger is that someone will assume otherwise.

The concern here isn't so much that of organizing around a nonconstraint—I think college and workplace readiness may in fact turn out to be a constraint, and that if we use it as the basis for organizing schools it may well subsume a host of other things now presumed to be constraints to nonstatus.

The problem is that we are again going to be guilty of organizing around a proxy for something. And since that proxy is itself a reflection of the status quo, we again land squarely in the problem we now have of reifying a status quo we are desperate to change.

SMALLER CLASS SIZE

A raincoat that doesn't have anything to do with testing is the smaller-class-size issue. Anyone who has picked up a paper and read an article or two on education in the last few years will certainly have come upon this topic.

The issue is pretty simple: a correlation was noticed between class size and the success of the students in those classes, and smaller class size indeed seemed to produce a superior result. Numerous policymakers grasped on to the correlation, assumed it was causal, and then imposed some version of it on the schools under their jurisdiction.

And some of it was indeed causal. Several studies have shown that smaller class size shows a benefit, but unless the reduction in class size is significant the benefits can be very minimal. In addition, another study suggested that smaller class size on its own does not cause much in the way of anything, but smaller class size combined with a variety of other supports can have a dramatic effect, most notably for populations that historically struggle.[5]

What makes class size a raincoat is the idea that a reduction in class size is *always* a good thing: the decontextualized interpretation problem. California and Florida assumed this was the case, and studies regarding their efforts produced a mixed result, while Tennessee, which reduced class size by up to a third and provided a full range of supports, saw an increase in broad measures of student performance that justified their decision to go to the expense of having smaller classes.[6]

When the small-class-size movement began, what should have been noted is that the wealthier the school (and this was certainly the case for private and parochial schools as well) the more likely it was to have smaller classes—and better equipment, more parents with time on their hands to better support their own children's success, more resources for training, less turnover of staff, and more—than those in poorer circumstances. Smaller class sizes were an artifact of a school's geographic location or mission independent of education, but to suggest that they were the cause that led to higher achievement ignores all of the other factors, many of which quite clearly would have a significant impact. When class size could be reduced in even the poorest of schools such that it freed teachers to be able to offer a similar set of supports as those in the wealthier schools, the experiment worked.

It has to be said that the policy community noticed the disparity between rich and poor schools, and again in a democratic act of kindness they wanted to extend the opportunities afforded in the wealthy schools to all students. Again, arguing that the motive here was wrong would be silly—what the policy community wanted was to increase the opportunity for all students to learn.

But then they passed policies that assumed a causal connection existed between smaller class size and student success for all students. They assumed that smaller class sizes somehow caused that success when a host of factors actually contributed to the ability to have smaller classes, and those factors combined with smaller class sizes certainly proved beneficial to students offered the opportunity to learn in such environments. But smaller class sizes absent those other things weren't likely to produce the desired outcome on their own.

In fact, one could argue that smaller class size made the whole system far less efficient, and it is difficult to see—other than in the cases where smaller class size had a real impact on schools that historically struggle—what other things that were also considered constraints were shown in the new organizing structure to have become nonconstraints.

Smaller class size, it can be said, is helpful, but the way the policies were implemented with a one-size-fits-all meant that complying meant expediting. Lots of new teachers had to be hired almost overnight, many with little experience in the classroom, and new classrooms had to be found in which to house them. Just that alone required an enormous influx of resources and effort, greatly increasing the cost of educating a child.

If you have to expedite in order to overcome a constraint, you are attempting to manage around the constraint, and you are making your system overall less efficient in terms of its ability to meet its goal. You may well increase the number of students that reach the goal for a short while, but doing so comes with a high price tag, and it isn't sustainable.

From a systems perspective, smaller class size should not be treated as a constraint but as a nonconstraint. This is because smaller class sizes do not cause success against the goal in all cases, which means that other things are also at play in determining that success.

This isn't to say that the smaller class size issue is unimportant—as I mentioned several studies suggest just the opposite—but that smaller class size on its own is a raincoat that makes it difficult to see that it was the adoption of a complete educational package that can make a difference, not a one-note policy. Yes, smaller classes make a huge difference for certain students in certain situations. Where that is the case, treating class size as a constraint for those students would allow the system to organize around those situations, which in turn stands a chance to make the entire system more efficient.

The nature of much of what we change in education is to increase the emphasis on a thing such that it causes us to expedite it for as long as we can and then revert to the status quo when the resources run dry. That does not get us closer to the goal of educating all students to a very high level—and ready for the worlds of college or work—in a sustainable way.

It is true that the smaller class size, college and workplace readiness, and Algebra II were all things that presented themselves as worthy of organizing around, but there are serious consequences for treating those things that are not actually constraints on the system—or in the case of class size, on the entire system—as if they were. Most notably, when we do that, we expect the system to produce more of the goal absent a structure aligned with the goal, which results in expediting the process, which makes things harder, less efficient, more expensive, and not sustainable.

My argument is that organizing around those things that are truly constraints is the way to create a system of education that is capable of achieving the goal. Then and only then will we avoid adding inefficiency and contradictory thinking to the system. It is imperative that we take the time to learn the actual cause of things, or we risk hurting the very system we are trying to help.

When it comes to the topics introduced throughout this book, what should be clear is that a host of improvements are needed. Our accountability systems are driving behaviors that are damaging our children's future, with a disproportionate impact on populations that historically struggle. Our standards take a form that historically has been used as a vehicle of control, not as the means to transform a system into something great. And our definitions of educational success within the established systems set a bar that is nowhere near the aspirations of those who coined the term *school reform*. The manner in which we talk about education has become so squishy that it allows for all sorts of incommensurability to coexist so long as the right terms can be applied.

Education needs a new way to change and improve itself. We already have a reasonable understanding as to the potential constraints that prevent more students from reaching the goal the educational system has for them, and yet so far our organizational strategies at the policy level have focused almost exclusively on nonconstraints. This in turn has made the system less efficient, more expensive, and less capable of achieving its goal.

I said at the beginning of this chapter that the really great news is that we already know how to organize the system of education around the things we believe to be important. The next step will be to organize it around the things that truly are constraints, to ferret out those things, school by school and district by district. Only by doing so will we ever stand a shot at a student's zip code no longer serving as the predominant indicator of what their future holds.

Policymakers may or may not come along for the ride. What I have presented here is a set of ideas that would certainly welcome an improved and more thoughtful policy environment but that can work to help schools improve regardless.

In the end, we have in front of us as a nation a daunting but worthwhile challenge. The fifty-five million students that enter school each fall deserve every opportunity to reach their educational goals, and it is all of our responsibilities to see that happen.

NOTES

1. Achieve, Inc., has been the primary supporter of policies at the state level that require Algebra II for all students in high schools. See their website at http://www.achieve.org/ for a description of that effort.

2. David Conley, *Toward a More Comprehensive Conception of College Readiness* (Eugene, OR: Educational Policy Improvement Center, 2007), 7.

3. Conley, 9.

4. From the Common Core home page: "The standards are designed to be robust and relevant to the real world, reflecting the knowledge and skills that our young people need for success in college and careers." http://www.corestandards.org/, accessed May 5, 2013.

5. Matthew M. Chingos and Grover J. Whitehurst, *Class Size: What Research Says and What It Means for State Policy* (Washington, DC: Brown Center on Educational Policy at Brookings, 2011), 6.

6. Chingos and Whitehurst, *Class Size*, 6.

Conclusion: The Birth of Something Great

Every child in this country is deserving of an education that sets him or her up for future successes. At the present the combination of our policies, our attitudes, and our overreliance on instruments and systems designed for entirely different purposes and circumstances are strangling our ability to keep that promise.

Our inability to change is further influenced by a combination of the fear that we might somehow make things worse and the lack of an approach to organizing the system of education such that it can work efficiently toward the goal of educating all students to a very high level.

I said in the beginning of this book that it was my goal to present an argument and a bit of a plan for shaking things up. We need it. I hope in that regard I was successful. I hope that what I've presented contributes to the formation of a set of theories that has far more explanatory power for how to create a great system of education that is a much needed improvement from the present set, which doesn't seem capable of explaining much at all.

Many years ago I had a conversation with my father that applies here. He was in a unique position at the time: as an adult with children in college, he made the decision to return to school and obtain an undergraduate, a masters, and a doctoral degree. It isn't often that a person is in graduate school at the same time as his or her parent, and it made for some interesting conversations.

At some point during those years when he was in graduate school, he called and asked me what I thought the product of an education should be. It was a bit of a strange question, but since then it has inspired lots of conversations.

My own answers veered from basing it on some body of academic content, to a particular set of skills, to definitions that attempted to position the answer in the student—such as an answer that suggests the product is a student with the capacity to have and to act upon a set of choices not limited by where they were born and schooled.

To this day I do not have a "right" answer, and I still talk about it with my father. I'm not sure I want to come up with a right answer, to be honest. I'm convinced that at the very least no single correct answer exists, and that the goal should be to constantly seek out a better answer than we had yesterday, and then get organized such that we can see those answers realized in our students.

What I do know is that the wrong answer is a student who can take tests and who can prove that they are on the top of the distributive pile as a result. If that is the answer, then we have failed in every way our mission as educators.

Our students deserve better.

Afterword: The Future of Schooling

During the course of sharing this manuscript prior to publication, several questions came up from reviewers that are worthy of some additional exploration. I've chosen to include some initial discussion in regard to them as an afterword in the hope that they take some of what I've outlined regarding a new set of theories regarding educational accountability and make them a bit more real.

I've chosen to treat them as an afterword because these are the type of topics that are worthy of a much broader discussion that includes lots of people other than just me. Thus, I'm willing to start the conversation. Just treat the brief snippets I include below as a starting point and not the last word.

The questions I've chosen to address briefly are these:

1. What will schools look like in five or ten years if we ignore what you say versus what they will look like if we pay heed to it?
2. How would you actually structure a school around its constraints?
3. How should we judge success in schools?
4. Can a behavioral standard be converted to a fulfillment standard?
5. I'm a parent of school-aged children. What can I do?

WHAT MIGHT SCHOOLS LOOK LIKE IN FIVE OR TEN YEARS?

Any time you attempt to predict the future, you should lead with a caveat: no one can predict the future. Crystal balls and soothsaying make for great bedtime stories, but they offer little value in real life.

However, I do think we have enough information to be able to prognosticate a bit about two future states, one in which we simply continue to do what we are doing now, and one in which we somehow manage to convince people in power that changes of the sort I advocate for can be made.

First, if we do nothing, then the present state of things is likely to be the future state of things. The present system, as I have argued, is designed to produce the very set of results it is now producing. It would make sense, then, that if the design remains the same then the results of tomorrow will look an awful lot like the results of today.

Consider what that means:

- The present unfairness in the status quo will continue to be the most significant indicator for a student's future success—education won't be able to trump the zip code in which a student lives.
- We will continue to have different standards for high- and low-achieving schools: high-achieving schools will be freed to pursue whatever they so desire, while low-achieving schools will continue to chase after higher test scores. This will further exacerbate the achievement gaps that currently exist.
- We will continue with the process of reducing the curriculum to the tested content necessary to pass the test and declare the student and the school successful, with a disproportionate amount of that occurring in the schools that historically struggle.
- We will continue to gather communities of people who use the terms of the day uncritically, which will allow those communities to continue functioning as if the contradictions in the present system don't actually exist. This will in turn allow for them to place the blame for the problems on teachers rather than a bad system.
- We will assume the existence of the perfect test score, one that signals college and workplace readiness and that all of the requirements of schooling have been satisfied, rather than realizing that no such metric exists. As such, the search for more appropriate metrics will be deemed to be unnecessary.

Of course, it will take a few years for all of this to come into perspective. The current focus on the Common Core and the Common Core assessments offers a beard of sorts to the problems, allowing us to put off judgments until after implementation is complete.

This, I think, is one of the biggest problems with the nature of our standards: they take half of a student's educational life to implement. If they are wrong, it will then take the other half to correct the problem, and then in the meantime we missed an entire generation of kids.

Now, for the hypothetical: What would a future state look like assuming my arguments are correct and those in power are willing to act on them?

Admittedly this requires a bit of speculation on my part, but with that as a caveat, here is what I would hope for:

- All students have as part of their repertoire an actual success story. All students will have written well, reasoned mathematically to a high level, and accomplished something significant and substantial. The fact that some took more or less time than their peers is irrelevant.
- Students have an opportunity to learn in an environment that is appropriate to their needs and not based upon a cookie-cutter approach to what a school is or should be.
- The quality determination for much of what happens in a school is returned to teachers, and increased efforts go into ensuring consistency in those judgments across the teaching force.
- Time is seen as the greatest constraint to learning, and the structures our schools take use that as a major consideration.
- Principals take on the responsibility of removing the constraints that exist by being given the authority to organize their schools around their unique constraints so as to avoid expediting the issues that exist.
- Standards take on the fulfillment role, rather than the behavioral role. The statements that are currently considered educational standards revert to their proper role of serving as curriculum guides. Each year of schooling is about students satisfying the fulfillment standards assigned to that year.
- Creativity is everywhere, with teachers and administrators constantly searching for new and better ways to help students achieve.
- Standardized testing is used as a research tool to understand what is working and can be scaled from one place to another. This can be accomplished via sampling programs so as to minimize the burden on schools. No one in a classroom pays any attention to it.
- Accountability is about the decisions a school and its leadership team make regarding what they will do to promote the larger goals of education. Those decisions will be combined with a variety of metrics to judge the performance of a school staff.

The exciting thing about a good bit of this is that it can be accomplished in spite of whatever the policy community imposes on schools—not all of it, mind you, but enough that it could make a real difference in a positive way.

School leaders actually have a surprising amount of flexibility, but it is hard to imagine even a terrific leader stepping out to support some of what I advocate without a community of support behind him or her. Without that support it would amount to professional suicide. With it, some marvelous things could be made to happen.

HOW WOULD YOU ACTUALLY STRUCTURE A SCHOOL
AROUND ITS CONSTRAINTS?

In chapter 9, "Fomenting the Right Changes," I pointed out that if we really want to be rid of the constraints in the educational system we have to be willing to organize the system around them. Otherwise, our only remaining solution is to expedite the issue in order to address the constraint.

The problem with expediting is that by definition it consumes additional resources (often lots of resources) in terms of time, money, and energy to overcome an obstacle that is in the way of reaching a goal. It doesn't help in raising the bar, nor does it allow for a more worthwhile goal. Instead, it adds cost just to maintain the status quo and to avoid falling further behind. It is a very inefficient way to get work done.

The good thing here is that schools already do both of these. At present, schools are organized around what many believe to be two constraints: grade levels and geography, and virtually all of the programs that schools implement in an attempt to increase the pace of the system and educate more students to higher levels are really forms of expediting. Thus, we already have a sense of what it looks like to attempt to organize around constraints, and we understand all too well the difficulties in expediting parts of the process.

Going forward, the challenge is going to be to organize around actual constraints that can then subsume the impact of those constraints to a negligible level. In doing so, it should allow us to avoid the efforts at expediting that we undergo now, which makes education a very difficult system to manage, change, or scale. It also makes it very difficult to create sustainable change, as virtually every change is a supplement to what already occurs, and as such it is always subject to available funding.

Schools are, of course, deeply governed in terms of their structure and what they are allowed to actually do, but I have been pleasantly surprised at the number of innovative leaders that have been given the opportunity to try new things.

Let's assume that we found just such a leader and just such a school. Here would be the steps we would go through in order to organize that school around its constraints:

1. We would look at the objective facts regarding the school's ability to meet its goal—all students leaving the school having achieved at a very high level. We would attempt to come up with multiple measures of the school's effectiveness (or lack thereof) that we agreed represented that effectiveness accurately.
2. We would then begin the process of searching for constraints and bottlenecks that are preventing us from fully achieving the goal. Noth-

ing at this point should be off the table *except* for those things that cannot be changed, such as socioeconomic status of the students.

3. Once we had a list of possible constraints, each of them needs to be explored to determine if it is a constraint or a nonconstraint. Is it something that if organized around makes that particular thing better but doesn't render a number of other possible constraints as nonconstraints? Or is it something that if organized around it suddenly moves a number of constraints to nonconstraint status? We must also ask if the effect of organizing around the constraint moves the school toward its goal.

4. We list the things in the system that aren't constraints but are not contributing to the goal—these need to be carefully documented because they are the things that may need to be reprioritized or, if possible, jettisoned.

5. Reorganize the system.

6. Track the metrics to ensure that the constraint no longer exists.

7. Repeat.

Let me be clear here that while I used the constraint of time in the chapter on change that I understand that overcoming that constraint is a systemic challenge and would require the full support of district leaders and perhaps even a legislature. Here, as a more practical example, let's focus on a constraint that could actually be managed by a principal and his or her staff: homework completion.

Much in the literature suggests that homework completion signals parental involvement as well as increases in achievement, and it may well be that in our particular school it was seen as a massive constraint, one that if we could overcome would subsume some of the other potential constraints to nonconstraint status.

An expedited approach to the problem would be to add after-school lab time for students who wanted a place to work and have teachers take turns staffing the lab in addition to their other duties. That would require additional resources, and as such it isn't a sustainable solution. When those resources are suddenly no longer available, the problem risks returning, and we're trying to get rid of the problem altogether.

Organizing around homework completion would require a realignment of existing tools and resources. In fact, it might even require that we forget about homework altogether and organize around parental involvement, which might then render homework completion a nonconstraint. A school that felt compelled to organize around such things would need to consider the population served, their available hours, parental obstacles to supporting their children, and so on, and then find a structure that worked for that audience.

It may be—if our school is in a particularly challenging neighborhood— that parents need some additional supports in order to help their kids. Or it may be that students need a quiet place to work and don't have one at home. It may be that the school is in fact in a middle-class neighborhood but for some reason has developed a pervasive culture such that homework is seen as an unnecessary option.

It could be any number of these or a myriad of others. It may be that the kids have jobs after school in order to help pay the bills and don't have the time to devote to it. It may be that the culture in the neighborhood is such that it doesn't value an education at all.

What have to be identified are the actual constraints and bottlenecks to getting homework done. And whatever we decide, the new structure needs to be sustainable, which means that something from the old structure has to go or at least lose its status as a priority. This is a trade-off. It is trading things that aren't helping the school move students closer to the goal for something that stands a chance. Teachers and principals already have full-time jobs, so it isn't fair or logical to look at them and suggest that the solution is for all of them to work harder for more hours each week.

Here would be two possibilities for organizing a school around the constraint of homework completion if it was determined to be a bottleneck to student success:

1. Devote an hour of instructional time on a daily basis to homework. This would require some very real trade-offs since a school would be sacrificing one thing in order to get something better—but if homework completion really were a constraint, then the trade would get the system closer to its goal.

2. Reassign a teacher from the classroom to a homework lab, or when a teacher retires use those funds for aides or other paraprofessional staff to run the lab and offer tutoring before school, during lunch, and after school. Again, this represents a trade-off. Those teachers that remain in classrooms will have to absorb larger class sizes, but doing so would remove the constraint and would thus be worthwhile.

Both are sustainable, don't require additional funding, and the impact of either is directly measurable. In addition, both avoid making the mistake of expediting the problem, which would make the overall system less efficient and require additional effort and resources. Expediting could actually be seen as a reasonable solution in this case because an after-school lab may be the ideal solution, but in that case you have to ask if you want a sustainable solution that permanently removes the constraint or an expedited one that strains resources and is thus always at risk should the additional resources not be available.

Earlier in the book I looked at the constraint of time, which I believe to be very real, but even if we never get the chance to organize around time every principal in this country has sufficient flexibility to look at the constraints in their school and do something about them.

If it is true (and it is) that each system in truth has only a small handful of actual constraints, and we can identify those constraints and organize around them, jettisoning or reprioritizing the things that aren't making a contribution in the process, schools stand a chance of creating some of the improvements their students need and deserve even if the policy community leaves the current system in place.

HOW SHOULD WE JUDGE SUCCESS?

In answer to this question, the words *thoughtfully* and *carefully* immediately come to mind. However, those are not really criteria by which a measure can be properly evaluated for its usefulness.

First, we need to provide the principal of a school with the same courtesy we do a CEO of a business when they present an earnings report. In effect, that CEO says, "Here are the decisions that were made for the following reasons, and now, here are the data elements that suggest we made a good decision or that we need to rethink a decision because it isn't panning out like we hoped." The numbers can then be cited as an indicator of the success of those decisions or the lack thereof.

The CEO then goes on to talk about the future: "Here are the things we will focus on over the next few quarters, and here is what we expect as a result."

In other words, that CEO and the leadership team of a company are held accountable for the decisions they make and the impact of those decisions on the company.

Schools are treated very differently. The newspapers across the country report test scores absent any decisions, and the accountability formulas as they now exist care not one whit what the decisions were that were made to produce a particular result.

In fact, the indicators that are used to judge schools—reading and mathematics test scores—are so far removed from most of the decisions that a leadership team has to make on a daily basis that it would be a true statement to suggest that an educational leadership team is held accountable only for a very small percentage of their overall decisions.

Every school, and every school leader, deserves to be held accountable for the specific decisions he or she makes. Each deserves the right to explain their decisions, show what was determined at the time of a major decision to be evidence that would show it to be a good or a bad decision, and then to present the evidence and suggest a plan forward. School leaders, I believe, have the right to be judged on the quality of their decisions.

And just like a CEO, there are some things that are just plain inexcusable. For a CEO, it might be losing money year in and year out, or decisions that lead to massive service failures of a product or repeated recalls. For a school leader the equivalent would be if the students entrusted to you were failing to accomplish the goal of education, which is to achieve (not on a standardized test) at a very high level based on a variety of metrics and evidence.

The quality of a school would thus be judged by the quality of decisions made by its leaders and their impact on the population of students being served, rather than via a proxy that has almost nothing to do with those decisions. That way, the definition of success that most of us have in our minds regarding what we want for our children matches the definition of success that a school is attempting to meet.

CAN A BEHAVIORAL STANDARD BE CONVERTED TO A FULFILLMENT STANDARD?

Asking how a behavioral standard might morph into a fulfillment standard is certainly understandable. After all, we have spent the last twenty years work- ing with curriculum guidelines (which are behavioral in nature: students should do this, read that, add those numbers), which have then been elevated to the level of a standard. If we could find a bridge between the two, or a way to transform our behavioral standards into fulfillment standards, that would frankly be ideal.

Such a bridge is not to be had, and here again we must revert back to arguments grounded in design. Statements designed to offer a guideline to the development of curricular materials and statements that define success within a system play such different roles that both are necessary, and one cannot and should not be made to substitute for the other. The differences at every level of meaning for both kinds of statements will allow them to function in a complementary fashion, with the curriculum guidelines serving as the basis for teaching that is in turn focused on the fulfillment standard that offers the target to be hit. However, those differences prevent either a fulfillment standard from taking on the role of curricular guide or a curricular guide from defining success.

Consider that at present the only way we have to adjudicate the quality of a set of educational standards in their current form are the subsequent test scores from a test derived from those same standards. That offers what is, by any definition, a closed system: you teach the curriculum dictated by the standards, students take a test based on content from those standards, the quality of the effort is judged as a result of those test scores, and you then adjust teaching as dictated by the test in an attempt to better align with the tested standards.

Where, in such a system, is the capacity to ask questions as to whether or not the standards contain the right things, in the proper order? Where is the ability to question if a more efficient or more appropriate path exists for particular populations, or if what is being learned is relevant in a broader context? None of those or a host of other questions can be answered because the system is closed. At some point the assumption was made that outside questioning of the system wasn't necessary and closed it off to such criticisms. Now, the standards-testing-accountability determination cycle repeats itself each year with very little opportunity to question the system itself.

An educational system that contains fulfillment standards such as those discussed in this book, and a set of curriculum guidelines, is a deeply self-critical system. The curriculum guidelines are only useful as they help students reach their targets in the fulfillment standards, and because a fulfillment standard is very transparent a wide range of stakeholders can judge its efficacy. At any point in time something that is not working should stick out like a sore thumb and force meaningful change of either the curriculum that failed to produce a desired result or the value of a fulfillment standard.

Thus, even if it were possible to convert a curriculum guide to a fulfillment standard I wouldn't want to do it. In education, both are necessary if meaningful, continuous improvement is the goal.

I'M A PARENT—WHAT CAN I DO?

The answer here is way more than you think. Schools are social institutions filled with idealistic people willing to work for less than most of them could make in the private sector. That is an asset that should be far better used by the public than generally happens.

As a parent, the following would help foment the types of decisions that will help a set of school leaders structure a school to get it closer to meeting the goal of education:

- Ask your child's teacher what they see to be the obstacles they would like removed to better enable them to do their job. If every teacher in this country was told that they could make a single improvement in their classroom that would impact their students positively and then had the power to make that change, that would represent a huge step in a positive direction for our students. Learn what it is that the teachers you know say in response to the question and start a conversation with other parents. That's how movements get started.

- Look for possible constraints as you see them. Chances are you'll see something. And once you do it will be hard to sit idly by while they prevent your child from receiving the full benefit he or she deserves.
- Spend an hour or two perusing your school and district's websites. Virtually every such website I've viewed contains the strategic plan for the school or the district, as well as progress on those plans. You should know what those plans contain and what the administrators of the school believe to be their priorities. If they aren't in line with what you believe they should be, you have the right and the responsibility to say something. If they have fallen into some of the traps I've identified in the preceding pages, you'll want to tread lightly. It has taken me almost twenty years to assemble these thoughts into their current form, and while most whom I share them with tend to eventually agree with me, they run up against precedent in a big way.
- Ignore whatever testing programs are in place and encourage others to do the same. Remember that a standardized test can only provide a valid set of scores if no one pays it any mind. Leave the use of the results to researchers and administrators, but encourage a thoughtful approach that refuses to base curricular decisions upon them. If you see anyone teaching to the test, escalate your concern until someone listens to you, and remember that the teachers may be doing what they were told, so don't automatically blame them for supporting an impoverished practice.
- Avoid the terms of the day. Don't get caught up in adopting a vocabulary that sounds as if it represents what you would want for your child until you have a full understanding of what it really represents. Surprisingly, a dictionary is the best tool for understanding when this has happened. When the meaning of the term seems to represent an invention that the dictionary hasn't heard of, care should be taken, because odds are no one knows what it really represents and as such it is probably masking a host of contradictions that need to be brought to the surface and resolved.
- Remember that the principal, the teachers in the school, and you as a parent are all on the same team. This is not an "us against them" mentality. Those teachers and the principal trained for their jobs just as you did for yours, and you need to place a good bit of trust in their decisions, just as you expect those who don't quite understand your job to offer you the same courtesy. I mentioned earlier that we often assume that having gone through school for some reason qualifies us as experts on education. That thinking is a fallacy through and through. Guard against it, and you'll have a better chance at making your point in a way that a teacher and a principal will hear.

Good luck.

Bibliography

American Educational Research Association. *Standards for Educational and Psychological Testing*. Washington, DC: American Educational Research Association, American Psychological Association, and the National Council on Measurement in Education, 1999.

Blackburn, Barbara. *Rigor Is Not a Four-Letter Word*. Larchmont, NY: Eye on Education, 2008.

Burke, Kenneth. *Permanence and Change: An Anatomy of Purpose*. Berkeley and Los Angeles: University of California Press, 1954.

Chingos, Matthew M., and Grover J. Whitehurst. *Class Size: What Research Says and What It Means for State Policy*. Washington, DC: Brown Center on Educational Policy at Brookings, 2011.

Common Core State Standards Initiative. "English Language Arts Standards Grades 9–10." http://www.corestandards.org/ELA-Literacy/RL/9-10/2, accessed April 8, 2013.

Conley, David T. *College and Career Ready: Helping All Students Succeed Beyond High School*. San Francisco: Jossey-Bass, 2010.

Conley, David T. *Toward a More Comprehensive Conception of College Readiness*. Eugene, OR: Educational Policy Improvement Center, 2007, 9.

Gardner, Richard et al. *A Nation at Risk: The Imperative for Educational Reform*. Washington DC: The National Commission on Excellence in Education, 1983.

Goldratt, Eliyahu M., and Jeff Cox. *The Goal: A Process of Ongoing Improvement, Third Edition*. Great Barrington, MA: North River Press, 2004.

Gould, Steven Jay. *The Mismeasure of Man*. New York: W. W. Norton and Company, 1996.

Koretz, Daniel. *Measuring Up: What Educational Testing Really Tells Us*. Cambridge, MA: Harvard University Press, 2008.

Kuhn, Thomas S. *The Structure of Scientific Revolutions, Second Edition*. Chicago: University of Chicago Press, 1970.

Leonhardt, David A. "A Simple Way to Send Poor Kids to Top Colleges," *New York Times*, March 29, 2013. http://www.nytimes.com/2013/03/31/opinion/sunday/a-simple-way-to-send-poor-kids-to-top-colleges.html?hp&_r=3&, accessed April 10, 2013.

National Commission on Teaching and America's Future. "Nation's Schools Facing Largest Teacher Retirement Wave in History," June 24, 2011. http://nctaf.org/announcements/nations-schools-facing-largest-teacher-retirement-wave-in-history/, accessed April 8, 2013.

Organizational Research Services. *Theory of Change: A Practical Tool for Action, Results, and Learning*. Annie E. Casey Foundation, 2004.

Parsad, Basmat, and Maura Spiegleman. *Arts Education in Elementary and Secondary Schools, 1999–2000 and 2009–2010*. Washington, DC: The National Center for Educational Statistics, Institute of Education Sciences, U.S. Department of Education, 2012.

Popham, W. James. "Why Standardized Tests Don't Measure Educational Quality." *Educational Leadership* 56, no. 6 (1999): 8–15.

Quaglia, Russ. "Student Aspirations: A Critical Dimension in Effective Schools," *Research in Rural Education* 6, no. 2 (1989): 7–9.

Riddle, Wayne, and Nancy Kober. *What Impact Will NCLB Waivers Have on the Consistency, Complexity and Transparency of State Accountability Systems?* Washington, DC: Center for Education Policy, 2012.

Rorty, Richard. *Contingency, Irony, and Solidarity.* Cambridge: Cambridge University Press, 1989.

Standards of Learning. Virginia Department of Education. http://www.doe.virginia.gov/testing/, accessed April 8, 2013.

Stillwell, Robert, and Jennifer Sable. *Public School Graduates and Dropouts from the Common Core of Data: School Year 2009–10: First Look (Provisional Data).* Washington, DC: U.S. Department of Education: National Center for Education Statistics, 2013.

Tanner, John R. "Missing the Mark: What Test Scores Really Tell Us." *School Administrator* 68, no. 9 (2011): 12–16.

U.S. National Archives and Records Administration. *Code of Federal Regulations.* Title 1. Improving the Academic Achievement of the Disadvantaged; Final Rule. 2002.

Index

absenteeism, as metric, 103–104
academics, standards and, 45
access: reform and, 15–16; to technology, as constraint, 138
accountability, vii; adaptive testing and, 118; assessment *vs.*, viii; in business, 93–95; business-inspired metrics for, 102–105; complexity and, 102; control and, 86; conventional tools in, xiii; cut scores and, 111; decisions and, 155; dimensions of, 91–92; in educational formula, 81–90; educational formula and, 88–90; equity and, 124; expectations and, 95, 125; leadership and, 100, 155; limits and, 99–100; overview of problems with, xiv, 79; package, 93–98; predictability and, 100; quality and, 86, 87; in reform, xiv–xv; rigor and, 25; sanctions and, viii–ix; simplistic approach to, 92–93; single-point-in-time judgments and, 82–83; synchronic judgments and, 83–85; synecdoche and, 92; teachers and, 13, 86–88; testing and, xv, 125; theories in, xvii; value-added models and, 108, 118–120
Achieve, Inc., 150n1
achievement: context and, 121; standards and, 40; testing and, 88; tests as proxy for, 71. *See also* success
Act Knowledge, 140n1

adaptive testing, 117–118
Algebra II, 142–144, 150n1
American National Standards Institute, 29
aphoristic standard, 36–37. *See also* standard(s)
arbiter of quality, 11, 13, 16, 87
art, 41
Aspen Institute, 140n1
aspirations, lack of, 138
assessment: accountability *vs.*, viii; non-test forms of, x. *See also* testing
averages, in statistics, 68–69
awareness, of paradigms, xx

behavioral standards, 39–51, 160–161. *See also* standard(s)
bias, test, 121
books. *See* textbooks
boredom, 138
Burke, Kenneth, 127, 141
business: accountability in, 93–95; metrics taken from context of, 102–105; schools *vs.*, 100

California Achievement Test, 55
causality, correlation and, 143
certification standards, 30, 31, 44, 45. *See also* standard(s)
change, systems for, 131
class size, 147–149
college, 89

CPSIA information can be obtained at www.ICGtesting.com
Printed in the USA
BVOW07s1944101213

338731BV00004B/5/P